HEBREWS

Chapters 1—7

J. Vernon McGee

THOMAS NELSON PUBLISHERS

Nashville

Published in Nashville, Tennessee, by Thomas Nelson, Inc., and distributed in Canada by Lawson Falle, Ltd., Cambridge, Ontario.

"Turn Your Eyes Upon Jesus" by Helen Lemmel. Copyright ©1922. Renewal 1950 by Helen Lemmel. Assigned to Singspiration, Inc. Used by permission.

Scripture quotations are from the KING JAMES VERSION of the Bible.

Library of Congress Cataloging-in-Publication Data

McGee, J. Vernon (John Vernon), 1904–1988
   [Thru the Bible with J. Vernon McGee]
   Thru the Bible commentary series / J. Vernon McGee.
     p.   cm.
   Reprint. Originally published: Thru the Bible with J. Vernon McGee. 1975.
   Includes bibliographical references.
   ISBN 0-8407-3304-6
   1. Bible—Commentaries. I. Title.
BS491.2.M37 1991
220.7'7—dc20   90–41340
                                    CIP

Printed in the United States of America

1 2 3 4 5 6 7 — 96 95 94 93 92 91

CONTENTS

HEBREWS—Chapters 1—7

PREFACE

The radio broadcasts of the Thru the Bible Radio five-year program were transcribed, edited, and published first in single-volume paperbacks to accommodate the radio audience.

There has been a minimal amount of further editing for this publication. Therefore, these messages are not the word-for-word recording of the taped messages which went out over the air. The changes were necessary to accommodate a reading audience rather than a listening audience.

These are popular messages, prepared originally for a radio audience. They should not be considered a commentary on the entire Bible in any sense of that term. These messages are devoid of any attempt to present a theological or technical commentary on the Bible. Behind these messages is a great deal of research and study in order to interpret the Bible from a popular rather than from a scholarly (and too-often boring) viewpoint.

We have definitely and deliberately attempted "to put the cookies on the bottom shelf so that the kiddies could get them."

The fact that these messages have been translated into many languages for radio broadcasting and have been received with enthusiasm reveals the need for a simple teaching of the whole Bible for the masses of the world.

I am indebted to many people and to many sources for bringing this volume into existence. I should express my especial thanks to my secretary, Gertrude Cutler, who supervised the editorial work; to Dr. Elliott R. Cole, my associate, who handled all the detailed work with the publishers; and finally, to my wife Ruth for tenaciously encouraging me from the beginning to put my notes and messages into printed form.

Solomon wrote, ". . . of making many books there is no end; and much study is a weariness of the flesh" (Eccl. 12:12). On a sea of books that flood the marketplace, we launch this series of THRU THE BIBLE with the hope that it might draw many to the one Book, *The Bible*.

J. VERNON McGEE

The Epistle to the

HEBREWS

INTRODUCTION

The Epistle to the Hebrews is of such importance that I rank it beside the Epistle to the Romans (which is excelled by no other book). I have wondered how to give this magnificent Epistle to the Hebrews the introduction it deserves. Before me are excellent expository works that other men have written, and I have decided to let four of them introduce this Epistle to the Hebrews to you since each of them makes statements that are all-important. They have said what I would like to say. First I will quote from G. Campbell Morgan's book, *God's Last Word to Man:*

> The letter to the Hebrews has an especial value today because there is abroad a very widespread conception of Christ which is lower than that of the New Testament. To illustrate what I mean by this, a recent writer has said:

> "One of the best things we can say about human nature is this, that whenever a situation occurs which can only be solved by an individual 'laying down his life for his friends,' some heroic person is certain to come forth, sooner or later, and offer himself as the victim—a Curtius to leap into the gulf, a Socrates to drink the hemlock, a Christ to get himself crucified on Calvary."

> I am not proposing to discuss that at any length, but at once say that to place Christ in that connection is to me little short of

blasphemy. We may properly speak of "a Curtius," "a Socrates" but when we speak of "a Christ," our reference to Him is not only out of harmony with the New Testament presentation, but implicitly a contradiction of what it declares concerning the uniqueness of His Person.

This is a tremendous beginning for the Epistle to the Hebrews.

Dr. William Pettingill, in his book *Into the Holiest: Simple Studies in Hebrews,* has a different emphasis in his opening statement:

> From Adam to Moses, through 2500 years, and from Moses to Malachi, through 1100 years, the prophets were speaking for God to man. But at the end of the 3600 years their revelation of God was only partial. Then after a silence of 400 years, when the fulness of the time was come, God sent forth His Son, and in that Son the revelation of God is perfect.

That is another tremendous statement.

Now I'm going to give a third introduction to the Epistle to the Hebrews. It comes from the excellent book by E. Schuyler English, *Studies in The Epistle to the Hebrews:*

> The Epistle to the Hebrews, one of the most important books of the New Testament in that it contains some of the chief doctrines of the Christian faith, is, as well, a book of infinite logic and great beauty. To read it is to breathe the atmosphere of heaven itself. To study it is to partake of strong spiritual meat. To abide in its teachings is to be led from immaturity to maturity in the knowledge of Christian truth and of Christ Himself. It is to "go on unto perfection."

And here is a further statement:

> The theme of the Epistle to the Hebrews, the only book of the New Testament in which our Lord is presented in His high

priestly office, is the supreme glory of Christ, the Son of God and Son of man.

This is tremendous!

Now I turn to the fourth author, Sir Robert Anderson, and quote from his book, *The Hebrews Epistle in the Light of the Types.* As we go through this epistle I trust I shall be able to emphasize this which he emphasizes so well, and I also trust that this introduction will clarify the thought:

> That the professing Church on earth is "the true vine"—this is the daring and impious lie of the apostasy. That it is "the olive tree" is a delusion shared by the mass of Christians in the churches of the Reformation. But the teaching of Scripture is explicit, that Christ Himself is the vine, and Israel the olive. For "God hath NOT cast away His people whom He foreknew."

This Epistle to the Hebrews was not accepted by the Western church for a long time, and the reason is found at this particular juncture: the church wanted to usurp the place of Israel. They adopted all the promises God had made to Israel and spiritualized them, applying them to themselves and rejecting God's purposes in the nation Israel. As a result, you'll find that the church in those early days became actually anti-Semitic and persecuted the Jew! Therefore, to say that God is through with the nation Israel is a sad blunder, and I trust that this episode may be helpful in our understanding the great truth that a Hebrew is a Hebrew, and when he becomes a Christian, he is still a Hebrew. When any person becomes a child of God, it does not change his nationality at all, but it brings him into a new body of believers called the church. Today God is calling out of both Jews and Gentiles a people for His name. When that is consummated, God will take His church out of this world, and He will pursue His purpose with the nation Israel, fulfilling all of His promises to them and through them to the gentile world in that day. I am indebted to these four wonderful expositors of the Word of God for helping us to get on the springboard so that we can plunge into the water of the Word.

The human author of the Epistle to the Hebrews has always been a moot question. Although the Authorized Version has the heading, "Epistle of Paul the Apostle to the Hebrews," there is still a question as to authorship. The Revised Version and other later versions correct this and simply entitle it the Epistle (or letter) to the Hebrews. If you are acquainted with the literature of the Scriptures, you recognize that there is no unanimity of thought and no agreement as to who is the author of this epistle. When I was a seminary student, I wrote a thesis on the authorship of Hebrews, and I attempted to sustain the position that the apostle Paul is the author.

When I wrote my thesis I thought I had solved the problem and that the world would be in agreement that Paul wrote Hebrews! But I find that there is just as much disagreement today about the authorship as there was before I wrote my thesis! Neither John Calvin nor Martin Luther accepted Paul's authorship, and neither did many others of the past. On the other hand, many do accept Paul as the author. However, the human author is not the important thing, but the fact that the Epistle to the Hebrews is part of God's inspired Word is important.

In spite of the fact that the Pauline authorship cannot be stated in a dogmatic fashion, there is abundant evidence that Paul was the author. Both internal and external evidence support the authorship of Paul. The writer had been in bonds (see Heb. 10:34). He wrote from Italy (see Heb. 13:24). His companion was Timothy (see Heb. 13:23). The writing is Pauline. Also, in my opinion, Peter identifies Paul as the writer (see 2 Pet. 3:15–16). I believe that there is good and sufficient reason for Paul's changing his style and for not giving his name in the epistle. I'll call attention to these things as we go along. (See the Appendix for a full treatment of the subject of authorship.)

The date of writing is particularly important in the case of the Epistle to the Hebrews because of the authorship question. Many scholars, even sound scholars, have taken the position that it was written after A.D. 70. Some give the date of A.D. 85, A.D. 96, and others up in the 90s. However, as you read this epistle, you are forced to the conclusion that the temple at Jerusalem was still standing at the time it was written. This means it had to have been written before A.D. 70, since Titus the Roman destroyed the temple in A.D. 70 and Paul had already gone to be with the Lord. I believe that it was written by the apostle Paul and it was written before A.D. 70.

Coleridge said that Romans revealed the *necessity* of the Christian faith but that Hebrews revealed the *superiority* of the Christian faith. This thought, running all the way through, is expressed in the use of the comparative word *better*, which occurs thirteen times. The Epistle to the Hebrews tells us that the Law was good, but that grace, under Christ, is better and that the glory that is coming is going to be the best. The Epistle to the Hebrews presents that which is better. The word *perfect* occurs fifteen times (with cognate words). It is an epistle that challenges us. *Let us* occurs thirteen times, and *let* occurs five times.

Two verses especially convey to us this "better" way: "Wherefore, holy brethren, partakers of the heavenly calling, consider the Apostle and High Priest of our profession, Christ Jesus" (Heb. 3:1). We are to *consider* Him. Then in Hebrews 12:3 we read the challenge: "For consider him that endured such contradiction of sinners against himself, lest ye be wearied and faint in your minds." That is exactly what we are going to do as we study the Epistle to the Hebrews. We are going to *consider* Him, the Lord Jesus Christ. I am convinced that that is the most important thing which any Christian can do.

OUTLINE

I. **Christ Better Than Old Testament Economy, Chapters 1—10**
   (Doctrinal)
   A. Christ Is Superior to Prophets, Chapter 1:1–3
   B. Christ Is Superior to Angels, Chapters 1:4—2:18
      1. Deity of Christ, Chapter 1:4–14
      2. Humanity of Christ, Chapter 2:1–18
         1st Danger Signal: Peril of Drifting, Chapters 2:1-4
   C. Christ Is Superior to Moses, Chapters 3:1—4:2
      2nd Danger Signal: Peril of Doubting, Chapters 3:7—4:2
   D. Christ Is Superior to Joshua, Chapter 4:3–13
   E. Christ Is Superior to Levitical Priesthood, Chapters
      4:14—7:28
      1. Our Great High Priest, Chapter 4:14–16
      2. Definition of a Priest, Chapters 5:1–10
         *3rd Danger Signal: Peril of Dull Hearing, Chapter
            5:11–14*
         4th Danger Signal: Peril of Departing, Chapter 6:1-20
      3. Christ Our High Priest after Order of Melchizedek,
         Chapter 7:1–28
         a. Christ Is Perpetual Priest, Chapter 7:1–3
         b. Christ Is Perfect Priest, Chapter 7:4–22
         c. Christ in His Person Is Perpetual and Perfect Priest,
            Chapter 7:23–28
   F. Christ as Our High Priest Ministers in Superior Sanctuary
      by Better Covenant Built upon Better Promises, Chapters
      8:1—10:39
      1. True Tabernacle, Chapter 8:1–5
      2. New Covenant, Better than the Old, Chapter 8:6–13
      3. New Sanctuary, Better than the Old, Chapter 9:1–10
      4. Superior Sacrifice, Chapters 9:11—10:18
      5. Encouragement, Chapter 10:19–25
         5th Danger Signal: Peril of Despising, Chapter 10:26-39

II. Christ Brings Better Benefits and Duties, Chapters 11—13
   (Practical)
   A. Faith, Chapter 11:1–40
   B. Hope, Chapter 12:1–29
      1. The Christian Race, Chapter 12:1–2
      2. Believers Are Now in Contest and Conflict, Chapter
         12:3–14
      6th Danger Signal: Peril of Denying, Chapter 12:15–29
   C. Love, Chapter 13:1–25
      1. Secret Life of Believers, Chapter 13:1–6
      2. Social Life of Believers, Chapter 13:7–14
      3. Spiritual Life of Believers, Chapter 13:15–19
      4. Benediction, Chapter 13:20–25

CHAPTER 1

The first section in this epistle is *doctrinal*. The first ten chapters reveal that Christ is better than the Old Testament economy. The second and last section of this epistle is *practical*, showing that Christ brings better benefits and duties. By the way, this is a pattern that the apostle Paul follows in his other epistles; that is, the doctrinal side and then the practical side. In my opinion, there is an abundance of evidence that Paul did write this Epistle to the Hebrews.

Although I cannot be dogmatic about the authorship of Hebrews, I can say very dogmatically that we are dealing with the Word of God—that which the Spirit of God has given to us. Because the Holy Spirit is unquestionably the author of this epistle, the human writer and the dating are secondary. The Epistle to the Hebrews is one of the greatest epistles we have in the Word of God. It is not pious cant when I say that I do not feel worthy or competent to deal with this great epistle. This is the reason I let four outstanding expositors introduce the epistle for me. From four different viewpoints each one came to this one point of emphasizing the person of Jesus Christ. Therefore I claim the promise of the Lord Jesus when He said that when the Spirit of God would come, He would take the things of Christ and show them unto us (see John 16:12–15.)

We need to keep in mind that this epistle is directed to Hebrew believers who stood at the juncture of two great dispensations. The dispensation of law had come to an end. The sacrifices in the temple that had once been so meaningful were now meaningless. What God had before required was now actually *sin* for a believer to practice, as this epistle will make very clear. The Epistle to the Hebrews is addressed to Hebrew believers, although its teachings are for believers of every race in every age. It is very meaningful to you and to me today. However, we do need to keep in mind that it was written to and for

Hebrew believers. For example, to say that Christ is superior to the prophets would be especially meaningful to a Hebrew.

CHRIST IS SUPERIOR TO THE PROPHETS

God, who at sundry times and in divers [diverse] manners spake in time past unto the fathers by the prophets [Heb. 1:1].

You will notice that this verse and this book begin with the word *God*. There are certain premises upon which this book rests. When you study geometry, there are certain axioms with which you must begin, and if you don't, you won't begin at all. If two plus two does not equal four, then you are at sea as far as mathematics is concerned. A straight line is the shortest distance between two points; that is a proven fact, and it is accepted. When that fact is established, you can move on and prove something else. In the Book of Hebrews, as in the Book of Genesis, no attempt is made to prove God's existence. Both books assume that there is a God. The Bible makes no effort to try to prove the existence of God. There are courses in seminaries today that try to build up some philosophic system by which the existence of God can be proven. I have been through courses like that, and I know what I'm talking about when I say it is a great waste of time. There is something wrong with you if you can't walk out and look up at the mountains, or go down to the seashore and look at the sea, or look up into the heavens, and recognize that there is a Creator. "The heavens declare the glory of God; and the firmament sheweth his handywork" (Ps. 19:1). My friend, if the created universe is not saying something to you about a Creator, there is something radically wrong with your thinking. As a young fellow said to me about an atheist, "Dr. McGee, he isn't dealing with a full deck!" It is the fool who has said in his heart that there is no God (see Ps. 14:1).

The second assumption we find in Hebrews 1:1 is that God has spoken. Realizing that God is an intelligent Person and that He has given mankind a certain degree of intelligence, if we didn't already have a revelation from Him, I would suggest that we wait for it. It is only logical that the Creator would get a message through to us. And the revelation that we have is the inspired Word of God. The first verse of Hebrews assumes that the Scriptures we have are divinely inspired. The revelation to which he refers is the revelation of the Old Testament as we have it today.

There are those who feel that Paul did not write the Book of Hebrews because it was written in such magnificent Greek. It was written by one who was a master of the Greek language. There is a smoothness and beauty in it that we miss in the English translation. Right at the beginning of this book there is a play upon two words. The word for "sundry times" in the Greek is *polumerōs,* and the word for "divers manners" is *polutropōs.* Notice the beauty of that—*polumerōs* and *polutropōs.* It is almost poetic—it sounds like Homer. But there is more than beauty; it is a tremendous statement.

"Sundry times" does not speak of time as we think of it. The emphasis is that God spoke through Moses, but before that He spoke to Abraham. He apparently spoke to Abraham through dreams and by sending the angel of the Lord to him, but when He spoke to Abraham, He did not tell him what He told Moses. God didn't say anything at all to Abraham about the Law. He did not give him the Ten Commandments, but later God did give the Ten Commandments to Moses. Even later on He told David that a king would be coming in his line who would be a Savior. And when David was an old man, he said that there was a king coming in his line who would be *his* Savior. God did not give that information to Moses, and He did not give it to Abraham. In fact, God gave Moses a law that Israel was not to have an earthly king because God would be their king. God, however, knew the human heart, and in time Israel wanted to be like the other nations round about them and have a human king. It was marvelous how God moved in a time like that. He granted their request, although He sent leanness to their souls. He used that as the method of getting the Messiah, the Savior, into the world. This first verse is telling us that God did not give all of His truth to Abraham, but added to it as He dealt with different men through the years. And in the fullness of time God sent forth His Son. There is a development of the truth in the Bible.

"Divers [diverse] manners" means that God used different ways of communicating. He appeared in dreams to Abraham, but He gave Moses the Law. Later on He made certain promises to Joshua. He spoke through dreams, He spoke through the Law, He spoke through the types, He spoke through ritual, He spoke through history, He spoke through poetry, and He spoke through prophecy. He used all these different ways over a long period of time, using about forty-five writers and communicating His Word over a period of about fifteen hundred years. The writer to the Hebrews is saying something quite wonderful to us at this point.

Have you ever stopped to think that the multiplicity of writers in and of itself makes the Bible a remarkable book? Shakespeare's writing was great on the human plane, but Shakespeare was the only author of his works. He didn't wait for a modern Hollywood writer to write any of his plays. (In fact, the Hollywood writers wreck Shakespeare's plays!) On the other hand, God used many human writers to write the Bible. He used men with different backgrounds and different abilities. One of them, Simon Peter, did not do so well with the Greek language, but I am not going to criticize him because I had nine years of Greek and I do much worse with it than Simon Peter did. But God used Peter, nevertheless. The writer of the Epistle to the Hebrews (and I believe it was Paul) was a master of the Greek language. When Paul wrote to the Galatians and to the Corinthians, he got right down where the rubber meets the road. He used the language that they used down on the waterfront, and Paul had been down on the waterfront because He traveled a great deal by boat. But his letter to the Hebrews is a work of art.

Oh, this epistle opens on a grand scale: "God!" There is nothing before it to try to prove He exists. If you deny the existence of God, the problem is with you, not with God. So many little men who carry a Ph.D. degree deny that God exists. My thought is, *Who are they?* Put one of those puny, little minds down by the side of God, and it becomes obvious why God did not waste His time proving who He is. If any person is going to come to God, that person must first believe that God is.

"Spake in time past unto the fathers." Who are the fathers mentioned in this verse? They are Abraham, Isaac, Jacob, Joshua, Moses,

David, Isaiah, etc. These are the fathers, but they are not my fathers—
and they may not be your fathers either. Obviously this is being written
to people who could call Abraham, Isaac, and Jacob their fathers,
which is the reason it is called the Epistle to the Hebrews. Nevertheless, He is God of the Gentiles also, and we can be thankful for that!

"Spake in time past unto the fathers by the prophets." A prophet is
one who speaks for God, and in the order of speaking for God he could
speak of things that were in the future. God spoke through many men
who were prophets, and they were tremendous men with tremendous
messages. It took all of them put together to give us the Old Testament,
but the best that could be said is that they gave merely a partial revelation.

But now we will see that God has spoken finally, completely ade-
quately, and assuredly in His Son—

**Hath in these last days spoken unto us by his Son, whom
he hath appointed heir of all things, by whom also he
made the worlds [Heb. 1:2].**

Now God has spoken finally through His Son—literally, "spoke to us
in Son." Or, as Dr. Westcott put it, "God spoke to us in one who has the
character that He is a Son." God has spoken through His Son. If He
spoke out of heaven at this moment, He would repeat something which
He has already said because, my friend, we have the last word from
God to this world in Jesus Christ.

"Hath in these last days spoken unto us." The word us is very important, referring to the same ones to whom He spoke through the
prophets in Old Testament times—Hebrew believers. You remember
that the Father spoke out of heaven saying, ". . . This is my beloved
Son, in whom I am well pleased; hear ye him" (Matt. 17:5). Since the
Father has given His final word in the Lord Jesus Christ, it is the final
word for you and me also. The Son is the One who is before us.

"Spoken unto us by his Son." Therefore Christ is superior to all of
the Old Testament writers because the revelation is filled up in Him.
He fulfills all of the Old Testament, and He Himself gives God's final
word to man. As Christ Jesus said when He was here over nineteen

hundred years ago, ". . . he [the Holy Spirit] shall take of mine, and shall shew it unto you" (John 16:15), so that the Spirit of God, speaking through John and James and Dr. Luke and Paul and Peter and the other writers of the New Testament, has given us the full revelation from God.

Now we are shown the superiority of the Son in seven matchless statements. None of us, I am sure, feel that we can comprehend any one of them completely.

"Whom he hath appointed heir of all things." The Lord Jesus Christ is heir of all things. Now this raises a question. In John 1:3 we read, "All things were made by him; and without him was not any thing made that was made." Creation is His, for He created it, we are told. It belongs to Him already, so how can He be the *heir* of all things? Well, He came to earth and took upon Himself our humanity. The first man in the human race was given dominion over this creation. We do not emphasize this enough because in Genesis tremendous statements are made in just a few words. Once, when we took a group to Israel, we had an Israeli Christian speak to us. When he came to the end of his message, he wanted to give an illustration, and he said, "I want to say this to you in little words." What he meant was *a few* words; he intended to make it brief. That is the way Moses wrote the first eleven chapters of Genesis—with "little words." He made it brief. When God says He gave man dominion over all the earth (see Gen. 1:26), He did not make him sort of a first class gardener to set out rose bushes and prune the plum trees. That is not what Adam did. Adam had *dominion*. Dominion has to do with rulership. All creation was under him. I believe that when Adam wanted more moisture over on the west forty, he needed only to call for it. When he wanted the heat turned on, he could turn it on. I think he controlled this earth; but when he sinned, he lost that control.

When the Lord Jesus came to this earth, He became a man. He performed miracles in every realm. He had control of the human body. He had control of nature—He could still storms, and He could feed five thousand people. He recovered what Adam had lost. The Lord Jesus is going to be *heir* of all things, and we are told in Scripture that we are heirs of God. Romans 8:16–17 tells us, "The Spirit itself beareth witness with our spirit, that we are the children of God: And if children, then heirs; heirs of God, and joint-heirs with Christ. . . ." *Joint-heirs* is an interesting word. It does not mean *equal* heirs. Let me illustrate that. Some folk have been very interested in our radio program and have given us wonderful support. They will mention us in their will. Sometimes we are mentioned as a joint-heir in the will, and sometimes we are mentioned as an equal heir. For example, a will might read, "I want so much to go to such and such a cause and so much to go to the Thru the Bible Radio Network." That makes us an equal heir with someone else. When an inheritance is left to us like this, we are free to do whatever we want to with it. But when we are a joint-heir in a will, it means that somebody else has the control of the inheritance, and they allocate just so much out to each one at the proper time; they manage the estate. Well, the Lord Jesus Christ is the heir, and we are just the joint-heirs. He will be in control, and He may put you or me in charge of a little something in the universe. In that way we are joint-heirs with Christ—we have an inheritance that is incorruptible, undefiled, unfading, and it is reserved in heaven for us. We have this inheritance because of the many wonderful things the Lord has done for us. He recovered what Adam lost, and even more than that, He has made us joint-heirs with Himself. Christ is the One who is going to inherit everything. As far as we know, no prophet in the Old Testament was ever promised anything like that. You see, the writer of this epistle is showing us that Christ is superior to the prophets.

"By whom also he made the worlds." Many people believe this refers to the creative act—"In the beginning God created the heaven and the earth" (Gen. 1:1). Actually, it does not refer to that at all. The Greek word here for "worlds" is *aiōn*. It means "ages"—"by whom He made the ages." This goes beyond His being the Creator. This lends purpose to everything. He is the heir who gives the program for the future. He made the ages, giving purpose for everything. Not only did He create everything, He did it for a purpose.

The Bible makes sense. God had a reason for the things He did, and He has a reason today for the things He continues to do.

For example, God created man and put him in a garden. He put down one condition for living there: Man was not to eat the fruit from a

certain tree. There was nothing wrong with the fruit; it was God's test
to that man to see if he would obey Him. (The problem was not the
fruit on the tree; it was the pair on the ground!) Man absolutely and
completely failed God's test at that time.

God has a program and purpose in everything. There came other
periods when God tested man. The time came when He gave man the
Mosaic Law. It, again, was a test of man's obedience. Today you and I
live under grace. We are saved by grace; we could never be saved by the
Law. Firstly, it wasn't given to us in this age, and, secondly, we
couldn't keep it. We cannot measure up to the righteous standard that
God has set. It ought to be quite obvious to every person that God cannot save us by works. He cannot save us by perfect works because we
cannot produce perfection; neither can He save us by imperfect works
because His standard is higher than that. Therefore God had to have
another way, and today it is by grace that we are saved.

The Lord Jesus Christ is the Creator of this universe, and there is
purpose to it. Abroad today is the idiotic notion that the universe is
running at breakneck speed through time and space like a car that has
lost the driver. The interesting thing is that when a car loses the driver
there is a wreck, but this universe, even according to the scientists, has
been running millions of years, and it has been doing pretty well, by
the way. The sun comes up at a certain time every morning; it is very
precise. The moon stays in a predictable orbit. As one of the men who
works on the moon modules says, all they have to do is aim, and the
moon will be there when the module gets there. You can always depend upon the moon. It is not running wild. The moon doesn't head
in another direction when it sees a module coming toward it. The
movement of the moon is absolutely predictable. This is not a mad
universe in which you and I live. It has a purpose, and the Lord Jesus
is the One who gives it purpose.

> **Who being the brightness of his glory, and the express
> image of his person, and upholding all things by the
> word of his power, when he had by himself purged our
> sins, sat down on the right hand of the Majesty on high
> [Heb. 1:3].**

What tremendous statements we have here!

"Who being the brightness of his glory." *Brightness* means "the outshining"; it means "the effulgence." The material sun out in space gives us a good illustration of this. We could never know the glory of the sun by looking at it because we can't look at it directly—it would blind us if we tried. But from the rays of the sun we get light and we get heat, and probably we get healing from it. That is the way we know about the sun. Now in somewhat the same way we would know very little about God apart from the revelation that God has given in His Son. The Lord Jesus Christ is the brightness we see. No one has seen God, but we know about Him now through Jesus Christ. Just as the rays of the sun with their warmth and light tell me about the physical sun, so the Lord Jesus reveals God to us today.

"The express image of his person." That word "express image" is the Greek *charaktēr*, the impressed character, like a steel engraving. We get our English word *character* from this. We say that the Lord Jesus Christ is the revelation of God because He *is* God. He is not just the printed material; He is the steel engraving of God because He is the exact copy, the image of God. Paul said in Colossians 2:9, ". . . in him dwelleth all the fulness of the Godhead bodily." How wonderful He is!

"Upholding all things by the word of his power." That little baby Jesus lying helplessly on the bosom of Mary in Bethlehem could have spoken this universe out of existence. He upholds all things by the word of His power. He not only created all things by His word, but He holds everything together.

Have you ever stopped to think about the amount of power that is required to hold it together? Man has learned very little about that power, but he has learned something. For instance, man has discovered the atom, a little bitty fellow. And when man untied the atom (they call it splitting the atom), he sure did release a lot of power. Who put all that power in the atom? Who holds all the little atoms together? The Lord Jesus Christ. He furnishes the program and the purpose; He is the person of God, and He is the preserver of all things. He not only created the universe by His word, but He holds everything together. If He let go today—well, since you and I are held on this earth by His glue, His stick'em, which we call gravitation—we would go flying out into space. He holds everything together. This universe would come unglued without His constant supervision and power. He is not like an Atlas holding up the earth passively; He is actively engaged in maintaining all of creation. As far as I can see, that is greater than creating it in the beginning. He keeps the thing running, keeps it functioning. This is one of the tremendous things He is doing today.

"When he had by himself purged our sins." The Lord Jesus Christ provided the cleansing for our sins. This, by the way, is the only purgatory mentioned in the Bible. He went through it for you and me; there is no purgatory for anyone who trusts Christ because He purged our sins. He has paid the penalty for them. How wonderful He is! The purging was accomplished by what He did on Calvary for you and for me. And today we are accepted in the Beloved. The one who comes to Christ receives a full redemption and complete forgiveness of sins.

"Sat down on the right hand of the Majesty on high." This actually is the message of Hebrews. The Lord Jesus received a glory and a majesty when He went back to the Father's throne that He never had before. There is something in heaven today that was not there twenty-five hundred years ago or in eternity past because in the glory now is the man with nail-pierced hands and the prints of nails in His feet and a spear wound in His side. Even in His glorified body they are there, and when we see Him, we shall know Him by the prints of the nails in His hands. Twenty-five hundred years ago He was God, but today He is the God-man.

"Sat down" does not indicate that He is resting because He is tired—or that He is doing nothing. It means that when He finished our redemption, He sat down because it was complete. This is exactly what the seventh day meant in creation—God rested on the seventh day. Was He tired? No. As John Wesley said, when He created the universe, He didn't half try. He rested because it was complete; there was nothing more that He needed to do.

Never, since I have been a pastor, have I been able to close my desk and go home with the satisfaction that everything has been done. There is always something incomplete—you should see my desk right now! My work is never complete, but Christ sat down because His work of redemption was complete. Friend, you cannot lift your little finger today to add to the redemption He wrought for us on the cross. He has completed our redemption, and we are complete in Christ. In Colossians 2:9–10 we are told, "For in him dwelleth all the fulness of the Godhead bodily. And ye are complete in him, which is the head of all principality and power." We are made complete in Him, made full in Him, and we are accepted in the Beloved.

The present ministry of Christ is another aspect of this. This, I think, was in the mind of the writer who said, "There is a man in the glory, but the church has lost sight of Him." His present ministry can be expressed like this: He died down here to save us; He lives up there to keep us saved. He has a ministry of intercession, a ministry of shepherding, a ministry of discipling His own. Although He is at God's right hand now, He is still vitally interested in those who are His own, and He is available to us.

My friend, what do you need? Do you need mercy? Do you need help? Do you need wisdom? Whatever you need, why don't you go to Him for it? If you ask Him to intervene in your behalf, He will work it out according to His will (not yours). Prayer is not to persuade God to do something that He didn't intend to do; prayer is to get you and me in line with the program of God. And Christ is at the right hand of the Father, ever living to make intercession for us. We can obtain mercy and find grace to help in time of need. This is the present ministry of Christ, and it makes these verses in Hebrews pretty real to you and to me. My friend, Buddha can't help you; Mohammed can't help you; no founder of the modern religions can help you. A friend told me of how he was healed by a so-called faith healer who is now dead. I asked him, "Can she help you now?" He retorted, "No, of course not, she is dead!" "Well," I said, "Jesus is alive. Our Great High Priest is alive today."

When we were at the Garden Tomb in Jerusalem I heard a thrilling story about a group of young people in Moscow who unfurled a banner at Lenin's tomb on Easter Sunday morning. The banner read, "Lenin is dead—Jesus is alive." Then they sang some resurrection songs. I don't know that anyone was won to the Lord through this, but it certainly was a brave effort on the part of youth, and their message is the message of the Book of Hebrews. "Lenin is dead—Jesus is alive." He is the

One who can help us. He is the One to whom we can turn. This is the great message of the Epistle to the Hebrews. When He "sat down on the right hand of the Majesty on high," He took with Him a glory that even God did not have, which was the body in which He had wrought out your redemption and mine upon this earth. He gave *Himself;* He shed His precious blood that you and I might have life.

CHRIST IS SUPERIOR TO ANGELS

Being made so much better than the angels, as he hath by inheritance obtained a more excellent name than they [Heb. 1:4].

Christ is superior to the angels. Angels were prominent in their ministry to Israel in the Old Testament. The law was given by the agency of angels (Ps. 68:17; Acts 7:53; Gal. 3:19). Cherubim were woven into the veil of the tabernacle, and cherubim were fashioned of gold for the mercy seat. We find that Isaiah had a vision of the seraphim. And in the Book of Revelation we find that after the church is removed, there is an angel ministry of judgment that is going to take place.

Now I say this rather carefully: angel ministry is not connected with the church. I know someone is going to say, "Brother McGee, after all, we have a guardian angel." Where did that idea come from? I don't think we have guardian angels. Some people say, "Oh, but we need to have a guardian angel." Let me ask you a question: "Are you a child of God?" If you are, you are indwelt by the Holy Spirit of God, who is the third Person of the Godhead. What could a guardian angel do for you that He couldn't do for you? Do you want to think that over for a while? My feeling is that the angel ministry is not connected with the church at all. This subject is becoming exceedingly difficult and dangerous today because there is a manifestation of demonism, and several writers are saying that demons are directing them—but they call them angels. My friend, an angel ministry is not for our day.

The idea of an active angel ministry in the church came about because some of the early church members who were marvelous artists liked to paint angels. I doubt whether any of them ever saw an angel, but they painted angels. If you have ever been in the Sistine Chapel in Rome and looked up at the ceiling, you get the feeling that angels are hovering over you. They are as thick as pigeons up there! They are everywhere. They are connected with everybody and everything. Michelangelo certainly did like to paint angels. Although I am glad that I've seen the Sistine Chapel, I wouldn't give five cents to see it again. I know that statement will be a heartbreak for some art lovers, but I don't care to see it again because it teaches the fact that there are angels connected with our lives today. My friend, *we* have to do with a *living Savior!* Let's just push the angels aside because we don't have to go to God through angels. We have the Holy Spirit, and we have Christ, our great intercessor. Let us get our minds off angels and center them upon the person of Christ. He is superior to angels.

"Being made so much better than the angels." The word *angel* simply means "messenger," and it doesn't mean anything else other than that. Angels worship the Lord Jesus. They are created creatures. Christ is *better* than the angels, and that statement is made definitely and dogmatically for us in Hebrews. In the Old Testament it is believed by many that the Lord Jesus Christ is referred to as "the angel of the Lord." But in the New Testament He becomes a man, and having assumed human form, He does not appear as the angel of the Lord any longer. He is the *man,* Christ Jesus. He is the Son of Man today. That is the emphasis of this Hebrew epistle.

Beginning with Hebrews 1:5 there is a series of quotations from the Old Testament; in fact, there are seven quotations, and six of them are from the Book of Psalms. The Psalms have more to say about Christ than they have to say about any other person. It is a H-I-M book—it was the hymn book of the temple, but it is all about Him; it is praise to Him. You have a more complete picture of Christ in the Psalms than you have in the Gospels. These quotations in Hebrews are very important. The writer of Hebrews quotes from the Old Testament to enforce his point, which is superiority of the Son over the angels.

For unto which of the angels said he at any time, Thou art my Son, this day have I begotten thee? And again, I

**will be to him a Father, and he shall be to me a Son?
[Heb. 1:5].**

"Thou art my Son, this day have I begotten thee" is a quotation from
Psalm 2:7. In Acts 13 we have recorded Paul's great sermon at Antioch
in Pisidia in which he quoted Psalm 2:7. Paul said that it had no reference to Bethlehem, but it referred to the *Resurrection* of Christ—when
He was brought back from the dead. Therefore, Christ is the only One
who could die for the sins of the world. No angel could save us, my
friend. Only Christ could become a man and pay the penalty, which
was death. "The wages of sin is death." He had to shed His blood, for
without the shedding of blood there is no remission of sins. Therefore,
He made that redemption for you and for me. Then He was brought
back from the dead. Why? Because He is the Son. He was *begotten*
from the dead.

"I will be to him a Father, and he shall be to me a Son" is a quotation from 2 Samuel. This is God's promise to David when He made His
covenant with him: "And when thy days be fulfilled, and thou shalt
sleep with thy fathers, I will set up thy seed after thee, which shall
proceed out of thy bowels, and I will establish his kingdom. He shall
build an house for my name, and I will stablish the throne of his kingdom for ever. I will be his father, and he shall be my son . . ." (2 Sam.
7:12–14). Now, there are those who say that this one in David's line
was only Solomon. Well, Hebrews 1:5 makes it very clear that when
God gave that promise to David it had reference to the Lord Jesus
Christ. I have heard arguments pro and con on this, but arguments are
pointless when we have the clear scriptural confirmation that this refers to Christ. He alone fulfilled it.

**And again, when he bringeth in the firstbegotten into
the world, he saith, And let all the angels of God worship him [Heb. 1:6].**

Now let me rearrange this a little: "And again he bringeth in the first
begotten into the world. He saith, And let all the angels of God worship him."

This verse is a quotation from Psalm 97:7 and Deuteronomy 32:43 in the Septuagint Version (though not in the Hebrew of the Old Testament). The angels of God are wonderful, but they are inferior to the Son. They are *His* angels, they are *His* ministers, and they are *His* worshippers. They worship Him, He does not worship them.

And of the angels he saith, Who maketh his angels spirits, and his ministers a flame of fire [Heb. 1:7].

This is a quotation from Psalm 104:4. The angels belong to the Lord. They are His ministers and worshippers. This is very important to see. The writer of Hebrews, who I believe is Paul, is showing that Christ is superior to the angels, and He is using the Old Testament Scriptures to prove it. Can you see how absolutely important the first two chapters of Hebrews are? They put down a foundation for the rest of the book which deals with the present ministry of Christ for believers today. Oh, that we might be conscious of the fact that there is a living Christ at God's right hand at this very moment! He is more real than I am because when you read these words, there is no telling where I will be. We just don't know what a day will bring forth. But Christ is going to be right up yonder at God's right hand for you and for me. He is the real, living Christ today.

It is easy to understand that angels were very important to the Hebrews because most of them were well acquainted with the Old Testament. They thought of angels as next to the very throne of God. They had read of the appearance of angels to many of God's servants and to many of the prophets. Angels were very important beings to them.

As I have already mentioned, I do not believe there is an angel ministry to the chruch in our day. I do not believe that angels appear to men. If you think you have seen an angel, you should check with your doctor or with a psychologist because you saw something besides an angel.

This reminds me of the two black fellows who met after not having seen each other for a long time. One of them said, "Are you married?" The other one replied, "Yes, I'm married." His friend then asked, "What kind of a girl did you marry?" "Well," replied the other fellow,

"I married an angel." The other one said, "You sure are lucky. Mine is still alive!"

Well, human beings never become angels. God has made this universe so that there are things visible and invisible. In Colossians 1:16 we read that Christ created things visible and invisible. For example, you cannot see an atom, but it is material and it becomes energy. God created intelligences that are above man. You and I live in a universe about which the Lord has said, "In my Father's house are many monē, meaning "abiding places" (see John 14:2). Created intelligences live in these abiding places, and God has created a great deal more in this universe than you and I could ever dream of today. Man did not come from animals. There is a material kingdom. There is the animal kingdom. There are creatures below man and creatures that are above man. We did not come from animals, and we will never become angels.

You may remember the song, "I want to be an angel and with the angels sing." When I was a little boy in Sunday school, the teacher would line up the little brats (I was the only good boy in the class) and have us sing, "I want to be an angel and with the angels sing." The last thing I wanted to be was an angel! And I still feel that way. I am very happy that the Scripture makes it clear that I am not going to be an angel.

The word angel (Gr.: aggelos) means "messenger" and may be applied to a human or divine messenger. There is an order of creatures that is supernatural, and we see that in the Scriptures. I think it would really surprise us if we had any conception of the number of angels in the universe. They are called the "host of heaven," and that means there are a whole lot of them. Their numbers apparently are not diminished or added to in any way, but we have no idea how many angels there are. They have an important part in God's plan, but Christ is superior to the angels.

> **But unto the Son he saith, Thy throne, O God, is for ever and ever: a sceptre of righteousness is the sceptre of thy kingdom.**

> **Thou hast loved righteousness, and hated iniquity;**

**therefore God, even thy God, hath anointed thee with
the oil of gladness above thy fellows [Heb. 1:8-9].**

These verses are a quotation from Psalm 45:6-7 which reveals that it is
one of the great messianic psalms. Psalm 45 tells us that there is One
coming in the line of David who will rule in righteousness. David is so
thrilled about this prospect that he says, ". . . My tongue is the pen of a
ready writer" (Ps. 45:1). David is saying, "I could *tell* you about this
much better than I could write about it." This One who is coming,
according to the writer to the Hebrews, is the Lord Jesus Christ. He is
the One who will rule in righteousness. God has not given the right to
rule the earth to any angel.

"Thou hast loved righteousness, and hated iniquity" is a tremendous statement. Imagine this old earth being ruled by One who loves
righteousness and hates iniquity!

"Thy throne, O God." This is God the Father calling God the Son
God! Do you want to deny that Christ is God manifest in the flesh? If
you do, then may I say that you are contradicting God Himself. God
called the Lord Jesus *God.* What are you going to call Him? I don't
know about you, but I am also going to call Him *God.* He is God manifest in the flesh. He is superior to angels because He is going to rule
over the universe. He is the Messiah. He is the King of Kings and Lord
of Lords who is going to rule over the earth some day.

**And, Thou, Lord, in the beginning hast laid the founda-
tion of the earth; and the heavens are the works of thine
hands:**

**They shall perish; but thou remainest; and they all shall
wax old as doth a garment;**

**And as a vesture shalt thou fold them up, and they shall
be changed: but thou art the same, and thy years shall
not fail [Heb. 1:10-12].**

These verses are quoted from Psalm 102:25-27. This is a tremendous
statement telling us that the Lord Jesus is the Creator. These are tre-

mendous contrasts given to us in this section: Angels are the creatures; the Lord is the Creator.

> **But to which of the angels said he at any time, Sit on my right hand, until I make thine enemies thy footstool? [Heb. 1:13].**

This verse is a quote from Psalm 110:1, a psalm that is quoted more than any other psalm in the New Testament. The Psalms teach the deity of Christ. There is a more complete picture of Christ in the Psalms than in the Gospels.

> **Are they not all ministering spirits, sent forth to minister for them who shall be heirs of salvation? [Heb. 1:14].**

Right away somebody is going to say, "Doesn't it say here that the angels are going to minister to the heirs of salvation?" Let's read the verse like it is. The angels are going to minister to those "who *shall* be heirs of salvation." This verse is looking forward to the time when God turns again to the nation Israel, and to the gentile world—*after* the church is removed from earth. Notice that it does not say that the angels are ministering to those who are *right now* the heirs of salvation. You see, God is moving according to His program, and He has a purpose for everything He does.

Christ is the Son; angels are servants. Christ is King; angels are subjects. Christ is the Creator; angels are creatures. Christ at this moment is waiting until His enemies will be made His footstool. The Father never gave such a promise to an angel, but He says that some day His Son shall rule. This tremendous section sets before us the deity of the Lord Jesus Christ and the exaltation of the Lord Jesus Christ. He is higher than the angels.

CHAPTER 2

THEME: Humanity of Christ

After seeing the exaltation of the Lord Jesus Christ in chapter 1, we come to the *humiliation* of Christ in chapter 2. He became a man, and when He did, He became *lower* than the angels. He was created a man in the womb of the Virgin Mary and took upon Himself our humanity. Therefore, Christ is the revealer of God, and He is the representative of man. We are going to find out two things about Christ in the Book of Hebrews: (1) He reveals God to man; and (2) He represents man before God.

I have a representative in heaven; I have someone there who represents *me.* I don't know about you, but I get the feeling that in my state capital and in my national capital those who are elected to represent me are not representing me at all. They are all out for themselves and their own little pet programs, and it doesn't make much difference to them what happens to the public. The only time they are interested in me is when I vote, and then I become the darling of the politicians. Then you and I are the intelligent public who cannot go wrong, provided we vote for them!

It is wonderful to have a representative before God, one who *does* represent us. It is good to know that we have somebody there for us because Scripture tells us that Satan, the accuser of the brethren, has access to God and accuses us before God day and night (see Rev. 12:10). Satan could tell God some pretty bad things about us, and so I am thankful I have a representative in heaven.

First we saw Christ higher than the angels because He is God. Now we see Him become lower than the angels. He was made in the likeness of man, and we see here His humanity.

There are *six* danger signals in the Book of Hebrews. They are warnings to the people of Israel that they fail not to enter into the full blessings which God has provided through Christ. These six danger

signals can be likened to highway markers to warn the reader. These
danger signals are as follows:

> Peril of drifting, 2:1–4
> Peril of doubting, 3:7—4:2
> Peril of dull hearing, 5:11–14
> Peril of departing, 6:1–20
> Peril of despising, 10:26–39
> Peril of denying, 12:15–29

There are two places in which a believer can live. He can live in the
desert and have a wilderness experience, or he can enter into the blessings of God by spiritually crossing the Jordan River. We find the example of this in Israel. God warned them at Kadesh-Barnea that they
would miss His full blessings if they failed to enter into the land.

Now I have literally crossed the Jordan River, and it wasn't pleasant
at all. I was on a bus that stopped five times, and by the time we got to
the Allenby Bridge I was so disgusted I didn't know whether I even
wanted to cross the Jordan River. As we drove over it, I looked at that
little muddy stream and thanked God that I had crossed the spiritual
Jordan in Jesus Christ through His death and resurrection. That is, I
had been buried with Him in baptism and raised with Him in newness
of life. That is what is meant by a Christian crossing the Jordan. Joshua
literally led the children of Israel across the Jordan. Christ *spiritually*
leads the ones who believe in Him across the Jordan into a newness of
life.

THE FIRST DANGER SIGNAL: PERIL OF DRIFTING

Let's realize that this is a warning for every child of God in our day
also, a warning that there is a danger of drifting.

> **Therefore we ought to give the more earnest heed to the
> things which we have heard, lest at any time we should
> let them slip [Heb. 2:1].**

Because this last revelation was superior to the Old Testament dispensation and came from One who is superior to angels, we are to pay particular attention to the warning. The responsibility is now greater.

"Let them slip" is *drift past them*. It indicates neglect, that is all. Neglect in any area of life is tragic, but in the spiritual realm, hearing the gospel message and doing nothing about it is infinitely more tragic. What must I do to be lost? Nothing!

The story is told of the man who went to sleep in his boat one night on the Niagara River. Before long his boat drifted down to the rapids and he was caught. It was too late for him to do anything. He went over the falls and was killed. Someone asks the question, "What must I do to be lost?" We are given the answer for "What must I do to be saved?" in Acts 16:31: ". . . Believe on the Lord Jesus Christ, and thou shalt be saved. . . ." But what is the answer for "What must I do to be lost?" Well, the answer is *nothing*. You and I belong to a lost human family. We are not on trial. I get a little weary of hearing that God has us on trial. He doesn't have us on trial; we are lost. Today He is saving some—those who will turn to Christ. The rest are already lost. You don't do *anything* to be lost because that is your natural condition.

There is great danger in neglect in every area of life. Many years ago I had a wonderful secretary who developed cancer of the hip. The doctor told her that she must have an operation, but she kept postponing it. Finally the day came when it was too late to do anything. She had been warned, but she just drifted, just neglected taking any action until it was too late.

When you move neglect to a higher realm, hearing the gospel message and doing nothing about it is infinitely more tragic. A great many folk hear the Gospel and give mental assent to it, but do nothing about it.

Some time ago a man said to me, "McGee, some day I am going to take up your offer and accept Christ." Right now, however, this man is drifting. I don't know how far along he is, but the day will come when he will be in the rapids, and then it will be too late—he will go over the falls. He may have a heart attack or be in an accident, and his chance to receive Christ will be gone. I would like to get all the folk that hear the

Gospel into the "now" generation. "Now" is the accepted time. "Now" is the day of salvation. There is a real danger of drifting, and Hebrews warns us about it.

> **For is the word spoken by angels was stedfast, and every transgression and disobedience received a just recompence of reward [Heb. 2:2].**

For example, when the two angels came to Sodom with the announcement that Sodom was to be destroyed, Sodom *was* destroyed exactly as they said. In fact, whenever an angel brought a message, you could depend on its being carried out just as it was stated.

Now notice the question—

> **How shall we escape, if we neglect so great salvation; which at the first began to be spoken by the Lord, and was confirmed unto us by them that heard him [Heb. 2:3].**

A great Welsh preacher began his sermon by saying, "I have a question to ask. I cannot answer it. You cannot answer it. Even God cannot answer it." Then he gave this as his text: "How shall we escape, if we neglect so great salvation?" Do you know a way of escape? The only way is Christ. He said so in John 14:6: "Jesus saith unto him, I am the way, the truth, and the life: no man cometh unto the Father, but by me." In the Scriptures we also read, "There is a way that seemeth right unto a man, but the end thereof are the ways of death" (Prov. 16:25). There are many *ways* that seem right to men. In California you can hear about as many ways as you want to hear. If you are looking for a religion, you will find one in California. If you don't find one that you like, you can start one, and I will guarantee that you will find some followers who will go along with you. There is a way that seems right to a man, but the end are the ways of death. How shall we escape, if we neglect so great a salvation? What do you do to be lost? Nothing. You can be lost by neglect.

"Which at the first began to be spoken by the Lord" is, of course, the Lord Jesus when He was here. He said, "Come unto me, all ye that labour and are heavy laden . . ." (Matt. 11:28) and "For the Son of man is come to seek and to save that which was lost" (Luke 19:10).

"And was confirmed unto us by them that heard him," refers to His disciples and others who heard Him and witnessed His death and resurrection—then went everywhere preaching the Gospel.

> **God also bearing them witness, both with signs and wonders, and with divers miracles, and gifts of the Holy Ghost, according to his own will? [Heb. 2:4].**

I think the writer of Hebrews has definite reference here to the Day of Pentecost when the gifts of the Holy Spirit were exercised. The gifts, of course, confirmed the message. To whom? To the nation Israel.

What tremendous truths we have here in this first danger warning. It is a warning sign, not about speeding up but about drifting—just drifting by these great truths which we may have been taking for granted.

SUPERIORITY OF CHRIST TO ANGELS
IN HIS HUMANITY

The humanity of Christ needs to be emphasized as well as His deity. You see, He brought diety down to this earth, and He took humanity back to heaven.

> **For unto the angels hath he not put in subjection the world to come, whereof we speak [Heb. 2:5].**

To begin with, let us understand what *world* the author is talking about. A great many folk think immediately that the "world to come" is heaven. However, the word for "world" in this verse means "inhabited earth" in the Greek. This verse is talking about the people of this earth. It is used in Matthew 24:14 which says, "And this gospel of the kingdom shall be preached in all the world [inhabited earth] for a witness unto all nations; and then shall the end come." It is also used in

Romans 10:18, "But I say, Have they not heard? Yes verily, their sound went into all the [inhabited] earth, and their words unto the ends of the world." The word *world* could not refer to heaven or to eternity. It does not refer to this dispensation of grace in which we live today. It speaks of the messianic kingdom, the kingdom that is coming on the earth. Hebrew believers, schooled in the Old Testament, knew that the theme song of that book was the coming kingdom over which one in David's line would rule. The messianic kingdom became the theme somg of every one of the prophets.

"Unto the angels hath he not put in subjection the world to come"—the millennial kingdom that is coming upon the earth. Not only have angels not ruled in the past, they will not rule in the future. They have been servants and messengers in the past, and they will continue to be servants in the future. This is the thought expressed here.

Now he turns to Psalm 8 and gives us an interpretation of that marvelous psalm which has to do with creation.

But one in a certain place testified, saying, What is man, that thou art mindful of him? or the son of man, that thou visitest him? [Heb. 2:6].

Verses 6–8 are a quote from Psalm 8:4–6. Let us pause here for just a moment. Who is man anyway? Man is just a small creature on one of the minor planets. Someone put it like this, "Man is a rash on the epidermis of a minor planet." That really puts man in his place, but I suppose it is more or less accurate. We are very small in God's universe. Someone else has said, "When you pick up the minutest piece of creation, the parts of an atom, and then you reach out to the largest, man is probably halfway between." Man stands about halfway in the physical creation, but the important thing is that the Lord of Glory, the second person of the Godhead, became Jesus, a *man*.

"What is man, that thou art mindful of him?" The answer to that is, "Jesus became a man. He left heaven's glory, came down to this earth, and He didn't become an angel." That is what the writer of the Epistle to the Hebrews is going to tell us. "What is man, that thou art mindful of him? or the son of man, that thou visitest him?" What is man?

Of himself, man is nothing. Physically, if you break down the elements of his body into chemical components and put them on the market, at one time he would only have been worth about ninety-eight cents. Today due to inflation man's worth is a little more than that. But it is not of much value, especially when you think of how much a dollar is worth. So, physically, man is not very valuable. Mentally, man thinks he is something, but he knows very little. What does man actually know about this vast universe in which we live? We have spent billions of dollars to send a man to the moon to see if we could find out how it all began. Since our nation doesn't believe the first chapter of Genesis, we are exploring the moon! Genesis 1:1 certainly sounds a lot better than any of man's theories. Man today isn't very much physically or mentally. He can't lift very much, and he can't do very much. Man is quite limited. When you take a good look at man, you see that he is a lost sinner. He is in terrible condition. What is man that God was mindful of him?

"Or the son of man, that thou visitest him?" Well, He visited us because He wanted to communicate with us, and He wanted to save us because He saw our lost condition.

> **Thou madest him a little lower than the angels; thou crownedst him with glory and honour, and didst set him over the works of thy hands [Heb. 2:7].**

God made man lower than the angels at the time of creation. Psalm 8 makes it abundantly clear that man was made lower than the angels. The One who was superior, higher than the angels, was willing to come down below angels. He became not an angel but a man!

Many of us believe that the One called the "angel of the Lord" in the Old Testament is Christ. I went across the brook Jabbok not long ago (Jabbok is in the kingdom of Jordan) and remembered that somewhere along that little creek (and that is all I would call it) the angel of the Lord wrestled with Jacob. That Angel of the Lord we believe is Christ.

We read in the New Testament that when Christ came to earth He became lower than the angels. Apparently angels are the measuring rod; they are the standard of the bureau of standards. Christ was above the angels, but when He became a man, He became lower than the angels. Why did the Lord do it? He did it so that He could reveal God. Also He is the representative of man before God. He brought God to earth and took man back to heaven. If you and I get to heaven it will be because we are in Christ.

This is God's original purpose with man—"Thou crownedst him with glory and honour, and didst set him over the works of thy hands." Man is going to do something that angels have never been able to do. Angels do not rule God's universe. They are God's messengers. There was an angel who attempted to rebel against God. He tried to set up his own kingdom. He attempted to become a ruler. His name was Lucifer, son of the morning. We know him today by the name of Satan, or the Devil. He was an angel of light, but he rebelled and said in his heart, ". . . I will exalt my throne above the stars of God. . . . I will be like the most High" (Isa. 14:13–14). God does not intend him or any angel to rule; but He has created man to rule.

Man, however, as we see him today is not capable of ruling. He is demonstrating this in all the capitals of the world—so much so that it makes me bow my head in shame. Man cannot rule, but he thinks he can—he has adopted Satan's viewpoint. He is attempting to rule without God. God could bless our nation today, as He blessed it in the past when men recognized their dependence upon God. But man in and of himself is not capable of ruling.

Because of making trips to England, I have studied a great deal of English history. I wanted to look at the abbeys, the castles, and the cathedrals with some degree of intelligence as to their background. I did not realize just how bloody the kings of England had been. The minute a man became king, he killed all his relatives so no one could take the throne away from him. If you were a brother or a cousin of a king, you were in trouble. He was apt to take you to the Tower of London—many a man lost his head there. Man, regardless of his race, is not capable of ruling this earth as God intended.

However, by redemption, God is going to bring man back to the place where he can rule. In Psalm 8 is the statement: "thou . . . hast crowned him with glory and honour. Thou madest him to have dominion over the works of thy hands." Man lost that dominion in the Garden of Eden when he disobeyed God, but Christ has recovered it.

Thou hast put all things in subjection under his feet. For in that he put all in subjection under him, he left nothing that is not put under him. But now we see not yet all things put under him [Heb. 2:8].

"Thou hast put all things in subjection under his feet"—whose feet? Christ's—not man's. "But now we see not yet all things put under him." Although our earth has not slipped out from under His control, He is not ruling today. When the Lord Jesus does rule on this earth, there will be no need of a hospital or a jail. There will be no crime or poverty. When He rules this earth it will be a millennial paradise. As the writer quotes Psalm 8, he makes it abundantly clear that the psalmist spoke of Christ, and the prediction is not fulfilled up to the present moment.

Now we have the very heart of this chapter—

But we see Jesus, who was made a little lower than the angels for the suffering of death, crowned with glory and honour; that he by the grace of God should taste death for every man [Heb. 2:9].

"But we see Jesus." Because of what the Lord Jesus has done, we behold Him. We see Jesus. This word see does not mean a casual look. The word means that we look upon Him with understanding. We recognize that in Him is something that our little minds do not grasp. We look upon Him in faith, in trust, in wonder, in awe, and in worship. All of this is wrapped up in the phrase, "We see Jesus." Do you "see" Him today? Has the Spirit of God taken the veil from your eyes so that you can see Him?

"We see Jesus." Notice that Jesus is His human name. At His conception the angel announced, ". . . thou shalt call his name JESUS: for he shall save his people from their sins" (Matt. 1:21).

"Who was made a little lower than the angels." The emphasis is not on being made lower than the angels, but upon the word *little*, and in that word the emphasis is upon time. We could say, "Who was made, for a little time, lower than the angels." For that brief time that He was upon earth (thirty-three years) He was made lower than the angels.

"For the suffering of death"—rather, *because* of the suffering of death. Christ alone could redeem man, and He could do it only by dying upon the cross. It was the *only* way.

"Crowned with glory and honor." He wasn't crowned with glory and honor by His death but because He came to this earth and died on the cross for you and for me. Let me emphasize again and again that there is a man in the glory. He wasn't there some twenty-five hundred years ago. Instead He was the second Person of the Godhead—let's call Him Jehovah, for Jesus is Jehovah. And He was and is God, very God of very God. But today He is also very man of very man. He took upon Himself humanity, and because He did this, He was given glory and honor in heaven that wasn't there before.

"Should taste death for every man" means that He not only experienced the pangs of death, but He had the experience of what death really is—the very fullest depth of it. He drank the cup of death. That bitter cup was pressed to His lips, and He drank every bit of it. He did this for you and me.

"By the grace of God." He did this by the grace of God—that God could be gracious to you and to me today and save us.

> **For it became him, for whom are all things, and by whom are all things, in bringing many sons unto glory, to make the captain of their salvation perfect through sufferings [Heb. 2:10].**

Jesus was not a man in whom God did something. The humanity of Jesus doesn't mean that He was a religious genius. It doesn't mean that He was a martyr to a cause. It doesn't mean that He was setting a good example. Christ's humiliation accomplished two things: (1) It brought glory and honor to the person of Christ; and (2) it procured man's salvation by making man's salvation possible. Christ took humanity to heaven, and there is not only a Man in glory, but there is a glory in that Man which was not there before.

"It became" simply means that it was fitting for Him—it was harmonious and consistent with His Person and purpose to bring many sons unto glory in this way. "It became *him* [the Lord Jesus] *for* whom are all things, and by whom are all things." He made all things, and they were for *Him*. If you want to know why this universe exists, it is because *Jesus* wanted it; it was *His* will. That is the origin of this universe—it began in the mind of Christ.

"In bringing many sons unto glory" is God's present purpose. God also has a future purpose of putting His King on His holy hill of Zion (see Ps. 2). God is moving forward with that program, but right now He is calling out a people for His name; He is bringing many sons home to glory. I read a letter a few moments ago from a young man who had sunk as low as one can go on dope and had spent time in prison. Now the Lord Jesus has saved him. We are seeing this happening all over the world. God is still calling out people for His name, bringing many sons unto glory.

"To make the captain of their salvation perfect through sufferings." The word *captain,* translated "author," appears again in chapter 12, verse 2. The same word is translated "prince" in Acts 3:15. It means "originator or leader." A captain is one who initiates and carries through. In other words, the Lord Jesus is the Alpha and Omega of everything. He is the beginning and the ending. He starts it, and He completes it. He is the Captain. He originated our salvation, and He consummated it. How did He do it? He did it by coming down to this earth and taking upon Himself our humanity. What did He do when He came to earth? He tasted death for every man. He came to redeem mankind and to procure man's salvation. He revealed God on earth, and today He represents man in heaven. We will see that when we get to the subject of His priesthood.

"Perfect through suffering." He was made perfect in the sense of being made complete. "Perfect" is from the Greek word *teleoō,* meaning "to carry to the goal; consummate; complete."

He was made perfect through suffering. Although He was the Son of God, and though He was God Himself, His perfect life does not save us. His virgin birth does not save us. Actually, His teaching does not save us. His miracles do not save us, nor does His example save us. But it is His death upon the cross that saves us. He was made complete; He reached completeness by dying on the cross. If you could convince me that God has decided to remain aloof from man, and all He did for this lost world was to pitch the Bible down here, and as He sits in heaven, He looks down on man and says, "It's too bad you are in such a mess; here is a Book, and I hope you can work your way out," then I am prepared to turn my back upon Him. But that is not what God did. He came down to earth and took upon *Himself* our humanity. Because He suffered and died upon the cross, I am prepared to trust in Him. I am prepared to love Him because of what He has done for me and all lost mankind.

> **For both he that sanctifieth and they who are sanctified are all of one: for which cause he is not ashamed to call them brethren [Heb. 2:11].**

"He that sanctifieth"—to be sanctified doesn't mean what the average person thinks it means. For many years I thought it meant to be a nice, sweet, little boy. Well, sanctification when it is used in connection with the Holy Spirit has to do with the work of God in us, to make us the kind of representative He wants down here on this earth. It is the work of the Spirit of God in the heart of the redeemed. However, sanctification when it is used in connection with the person of Christ (as in this Epistle to the Hebrews) is not purification. It is not a *condition* but a *position* that we have in Christ. He was the Just One who took the place of the unjust that He might bring us to God. And He has brought us now into the family of God.

"For which cause he is not ashamed to call them brethren." In the family of God, He is not ashamed to call us brothers. Now, of course, I would not dare call Him brother, but *He* has brought us into the family of God. He is the firstborn among many brethren; He is the *head* of the family, and He calls us brethren because we all become sons of God through faith in the Lord Jesus Christ.

My friend, this makes it very clear that the heresy about the universal fatherhood of God and the universal brotherhood of man is entirely false. It is probably the most damnable doctrine there is abroad today.

Saying, I will declare thy name unto my brethren, in the midst of the church will I sing praise unto thee [Heb. 2:12].

This verse is a quotation from Psalm 22, the great psalm of the cross. The first part of Psalm 22 denotes the humiliation of Christ, and you actually are given the seven last words of Christ on the cross. Beginning with verse 22 of the psalm you have the exaltation of Christ: "I will declare thy name unto my brethren: in the midst of the congregation will I praise thee" (Ps. 22:22). I am of the opinion that we could restrict this verse to the Hebrew brethren because it was written to the Jews.

"In the midst of the church will I sing praise unto thee." The word *church* is "congregation" rather than the technical meaning of the word *church*.

Now here is another quotation from the Old Testament, Isaiah 8:17–18.

And again, I will put my trust in him. And again, Behold I and the children which God hath given me [Heb. 2:13].

This verse reveals how the Holy Spirit interprets Scripture. There are those today who try to give an interpretation of the prophets that eliminates any reference to Jesus Christ at all. In fact, when I read Isaiah 8:17–18, it seems that the writer is talking about the sons of Isaiah, at least that is the way I understand it. But here in verse 13 the Holy Spirit of God interprets that reference in Isaiah in such a way that it refers to the Lord Jesus Christ. Anyone today who attempts to eliminate the Lord Jesus from the prophets, therefore, is contradicting the interpretation that the Holy Spirit has given in the New Testament.

You will remember that when the Lord Jesus came back from the dead He said, ". . . go to my brethren, and say unto them, I ascend unto my Father, and your Father; and to my God, and your God" (John 20:17). When Jesus said, "Go to my brethren," He was referring to His apostles at that particular time, and they were, of course, all Jewish. I emphasize this because I think it is very important to keep before us the ones to whom this epistle was written. It will enable me to give a correct interpretation that, I trust, might lead to an application to your heart and to my heart.

> **Forasmuch then as the children are partakers of flesh and blood, he also himself likewise took part of the same; that through death he might destroy him that had the power of death, that is, the devil [Heb. 2:14].**

This statement emphasizes the Lord's incarnation.

"As the children are partakers of flesh and blood, he also himself likewise took part of the same." Christ came in a way they were not expecting Him to come. However, they should have known because the prophets had made clear the way He would come to earth the first time. As George Macdonald put it:

> They were looking for a King
> To slay their foes and lift them high;
> Thou cam'st, a little baby thing
> That made a woman cry.

Because we were made of flesh and blood, He took upon Himself flesh and blood. And He came into this world by human birth just like you and I came into the world.

"That through death he might destroy him." Christ Jesus came not only through birth—His birth didn't save anyone—but through death. It is by His death He saves us, not by His birth or by His life. His death brought to us salvation and deliverance from spiritual and eternal death.

> **And deliver them who through fear of death were all their lifetime subject to bondage [Heb. 2:15].**

In my opinion, E. Schuyler English (*Studies in the Epistle to the Hebrews*, p. 82) has the correct interpretation of this verse:

> The Law of God demanded and does demand death for sin. "The soul that sinneth, it shall die." "The wages of sin is death." Satan was the cause of man's sin in the first place and, even though he is a usurper, he can claim, justly so in a sense, that the sinner must die. He had the power, the authority to demand that every sinner should pay sin's penalty. And on account of this all men, because all are sinners, were fearful of death and subject to bondage, because of sin, to serve it and thus serve Satan.

For verily he took not on him the nature of angels; but he took on him the seed of Abraham [Heb. 2:16].

In the Old Testament Christ took on the nature of angels. He did that when He appeared as the Angel of the Lord, and these Hebrews understood that. When Christ left heaven and came to earth, He came past the angels and came to fallen man. He took on Him the seed of Abraham. He came in the line of Abraham. God began the preparation at the very beginning with Adam and Eve. At that time God said that there would come the seed of the woman (see Gen. 3:15). Then God said He would come in the line of Abraham, and a little farther along we learn that He would be born in the tribe of Judah, of the family of David, of the nation Israel. He was to be born of a virgin. The Lord put up enough highway markers so that everybody—not only wise men, but everybody—should have found their way to Bethlehem when Jesus was born.

Wherefore in all things it behoved him to be made like unto his brethren, that he might be a merciful and faithful high priest in things pertaining to God, to make reconciliation for the sins of the people [Heb. 2:17].

The Lord Jesus came down to earth in the likeness of men. In Philippians 2:7 we read, "But made himself of no reputation, and took upon him the form of a servant, and was made in the likeness of men." It was a real likeness to men. This likeness, Vincent tells us, is "closest where the traces of the curse of sin were more apparent—in poverty, temptation, and violent and unmerited death." Christ could have been born in the palace of Caesar, but He was born in real poverty, in a stable behind an inn. Why? So that He could know something of the effect of sin on humanity. Where do you see it? You see it in poverty. You see it in temptation. You see it in violent and unmerited death. That is where you see sin manifested.

I think it is tragic when innocent people suffer. Some time ago in Pasadena a dear, talented, Christian woman, an outstanding artist up in her 80s, was followed home by a teenager who cruelly and brutally murdered her. How terrible it was! And nothing was done about it. Thank God, He is going to make things right some day.

When Christ came to earth, He knew what real poverty was. During World War II, I went through El Paso, Texas, on the train. Before the train pulled into the station, the conductor came by and said, "Don't get off the train because there are people in this station who have been there for a week and cannot get out. They are desperate. If you leave your seat, one of them will take it and you will never get it back. Stay right where you are." We did what he said, but once the train started its journey again, I searched out the conductor and asked him what it was all about. He told me that many of those people were camping in the station, waiting for a seat on a train. Remember, this was during the war, and many men were being shipped overseas. One young woman told the conductor that her husband had been shipped out and she was stranded. She couldn't get back to her people; so she was just waiting in the station. He also told me that a little boy had been born in that station the other night. Imagine being born in a station! The little fellow is a great big fellow now, and I sure hope someone has told him about Jesus because He also was born in a crush like that when there was a great movement of humanity. You recall that it was Caesar who made a tax bill requiring that every person under the domain of Rome be enrolled in their hometown for taxing. Mary *had* to go to Bethlehem although it was near the time for her baby to be born. When she got to Bethlehem, there was no room in the inn, and so the

Lord Jesus Christ was born in a stable. He could sympathize with that baby born in El Paso's Union Station, couldn't He?

The Lord Jesus came to earth and took on a human body. He is able to sympathize with you and me. I don't care who you are or where you are, He knows you and He understands you—not just because He is God, but because He became a man. He knows exactly what you and I are going through today.

At the time this book is being written there is a great deal of poverty in the Middle East, especially among the Arabs. My heart goes out to the refugees there. We cannot condone their rash acts and murder which they have committed, but do you know that some of them have been living in those wretched camps since 1948? Their living conditions are absolutely horrible. Even their own brethren, the other Arabs, have not permitted them to integrate among their people. They have been confined to these camps. Well, there was wretched poverty in the Middle East when Jesus lived there. And "it behoved him to be made like unto his brethren." He came in poverty. The poverty of Jesus' family is almost unspeakable. He was born into a race that was under the heel of Rome; they were in subjection to Rome. He wasn't born in a palace; He was born in a stable. He was in all points made like unto His brethren. He became one of them. If you had seen that little boy playing in Bethlehem, wearing a little ragged garment, you would not have known who He was. When the artist paints Him, He stands out like a bright cameo, but He was probably just a dirty-faced little boy, not any different in appearance from His playmates. He was made like unto His brethren.

In emphasizing the deity of Christ there is a danger of underestimating His humanity. I am happy that I was not born in Bethlehem. I am delighted that I was not raised in Nazareth. I want to tell you that even today the children in those towns don't have much of a chance. Just think of what it was like in Jesus' day! Jesus Christ became a real human being, and He came out of that background. He was a root out of a dry ground. You have never had a thought nor have you ever suffered anything that He doesn't already know about. For this reason He can be a merciful and faithful High Priest.

"That he might be a merciful and faithful high priest in things pertaining to God, to make reconciliation for the sins of the people." It is more accurate to say "to make *propitiation*," rather than "reconciliation." Christ made a mercy seat for you and me to come to. And, my friend, what we need is *mercy*. God has a great deal of it available to us because Jesus made a mercy seat, and you can go there and get all you need. I don't know about you, but I need a whole lot of it, and after I have used up a great deal of it, there is still plenty of it for you today. Christ made a mercy seat for the *sins of the people*, and that is the only place you can get God's mercy.

> **For in that he himself hath suffered being tempted, he is able to succour them that are tempted [Heb. 2:18].**

"For in that he himself hath suffered being tempted"—the word should be *tested*. The Lord Jesus was tested, not only for forty days (that was a testing in a particular way), but during His entire life He was tested.

I want to look closely at this verse because some of you are going to disagree with what I am going to say about it. The question is asked concerning the testing of Jesus, "Could He have succumbed to the temptation? Could He have fallen?" The answer is *no*. When we speak of being tempted to do something wrong, what we actually mean is that we have the *opportunity* to do wrong, and we want to do it. Now the opportunity was the testing, but the desire to do wrong was sin, and a sinful *desire* is itself sin. The Lord Jesus never had that sinful desire. He was not a sinner, but He certainly had the opportunity. Knowing how hungry and weak He was from going without food for forty days, Satan began his temptation by saying, "Why don't you make these rocks into bread?" If you have been to that land, you know that there are a whole lot of rocks there! That was the temptation. He *could* have made stones into bread, but He didn't. His test was greater than mine. I want you to know that if I could make stones into bread I'd be in the bakery business! He could have, but He didn't. He had the opportunity to do it, and that is the test. He did not yield to it. He did not desire to yield to the test; and he could not so desire because of the very fact that He was God.

Again I ask the question: Could Jesus have sinned? The answer is no, He could not have sinned. What then was the purpose of the testing? I feel that I can answer that best with an illustration.

When I was a boy, I lived in West Texas on the east fork of the Brazos River. In the summertime there wasn't enough water in the river to rust a shingle nail, but in the wintertime you could have floated a battleship down there. The little town has disappeared now, but when I lived there, the Santa Fe Railroad went through it and across the Brazos River. One winter we had a flood that washed out the railroad bridge—it was a wooden bridge. So the railroad company came in and replaced it with a steel bridge. When it was completed, they brought two engines to our town, stopped them on top of the new bridge, and tied down their whistles. Well, nobody in our little town had ever heard two whistles at one time, so we all rushed down to the bridge—all twenty-seven of us. We stood there watching, and one of the extroverts of our town asked the engineer, "What are you doing?" He said, "We are testing the bridge." So he asked, "Do you think it will fall down?" With a sneer, the engineer said, "Of course it won't fall down!" "Then why are you doing this?" This was the engineer's answer: "We are putting these two engines there to *prove* that it won't fall down."

Jesus, you see, was tested to *prove* that He was who He claimed to be. That is very important. Actually, if Jesus of Nazareth had sinned, it would not have proven that God in the flesh could sin. Rather, it would have proven that Jesus of Nazareth was not God in the flesh. The testing proved that He was God in the flesh. Because of who He is, He cannot sin. And the writer of the Hebrew epistle adds that He was tested in all points like we are, yet was without sin (see Heb. 4:15).

"For in that he himself hath suffered being tempted, he is able to succour them that are tempted." The word *succour* means, of course, "to come to the aid of, help, assist." Because He suffered being tempted, He is able to help others who are tested. As we get further along in this epistle, we will be studying the priesthood of God. We will see that the Lord Jesus Christ is able to help those who are tested. If there is one thing I hope this study in the Book of Hebrews will achieve, it is to make you and me very conscious that we have an High

Priest. He is alive at this moment. He is at God's right hand, and, best of all, He is available to us. When I wake up in the dark watches of the night and toss and turn, as I sometimes do, with some burden on my heart, I can look up. My High Priest is up there. He knows me, He understands, and I can take my burden to Him. When that dark moment comes, and you and I go down into the valley of the shadow of death, we have a great High Priest up yonder who will help us. No matter what happens, no matter what the test, He is able to help us. I am afraid that we do not use His services as we should. We forget about Him and try to fight our battles alone. My friend, He is available. He wants you to come to Him.

CHAPTER 3

THEME: Christ is superior to Moses

We have already seen that Christ is superior to the prophets, and we have just concluded the section which proves Him to be superior to the angels. Now we will see that He is superior to Moses.

Wherefore, holy brethren, partakers of the heavenly calling, consider the Apostle and High Priest of our profession, Christ Jesus [Heb. 3:1].

This chapter begins with the word *Wherefore,* and this is another reason I feel that Paul is the author of this epistle. Paul used the words *wherefore* and *therefore* as sort of a hinge or cement to present that which is logical. Now in the verse before us, *wherefore* is even more than that. It is like a swinging door which goes back and forth both ways. Or it can be looked at as a marker when you come in on a freeway or come in on a main thoroughfare. The warning is, "Look both ways." The word *wherefore* looks back at what the writer has already said, and it looks forward to what he will say.

"Wherefore, holy brethren." The word *brethren* means those who were Hebrews like Paul was. Paul after the flesh was a Hebrew. He called the Jews his brethren after the flesh. They are called "holy" brethren in this verse, not because of the things they did, but because the word *holy* means "separated"—they were separated unto God. They belonged to Him.

"Partakers of the heavenly calling." The nation Israel had an earthly calling. All the promises of the Old Testament given to Israel had to do with this earth. He promised them rain from heaven; He promised them fertility of the soil and bountiful crops. These are physical blessings, although He promised them spiritual blessings as well. Today the idea that anything physical cannot be used in a spiritual way is wrong. That is one reason people don't like to have money mentioned in church. What is wrong with money? It can be used in a spiritual way; it is not very impressive to hear somebody pray for something and then not back it up with his pocketbook. For example, if you are going to pray for missions, I would suggest you give to missions if you want to make your prayer effective. Otherwise your prayer is just like a lot of wind escaping—that's all. It is spiritual to give; that is one of the ministries a priest performs. He offers up spiritual sacrifices. Giving is one of them, and the praise of our lips is another.

The brethren who are partakers of the heavenly calling previously had an earthly calling, but now they have come up to date and they belong to the "now" generation of those of Israel who have turned to Christ. The writer to the Hebrews will be making it very clear that they have moved into a different age. In the past they offered animal sacrifices according to the Mosaic system, and it was right to do so. But now it is wrong because the sacrificial system has all been fulfilled in Christ, and they have a heavenly calling. The earthly calling hasn't disappeared, but it has been changed for the heavenly calling—so that they are partakers of the heavenly calling.

Several missionaries in Israel try to make this clear to us in our day. When witnessing to a Jew we tend to give the impression that he will have to cease being a Jew. I don't know why we do this. A man can still be a Jew and be a Christian. If we are German, English, or French, we are still that when we become a child of God. Nobody asks us to give up our nationality. And the Jew is still a Jew after he has come to Christ. He has moved along with the revelation of God, and he is a partaker now of the heavenly calling. This is important to see. The Epistle to the Hebrews becomes almost meaningless if you don't consider to whom it was written—and also when it was written.

Someone sent me John Wycliffe's *Golden Rule of Interpretation*. John Wycliffe lived from 1324 to 1380, and although that was a long time ago, I think his Golden Rule is still gold; it is not tarnished at all. Listen to his Golden Rule:

It shall greatly help thee to understand Scripture if thou mark not only what is spoken or written, but of whom and to whom, with what words, at what time, where, and to what intent, under what circumstances, considering what goeth before and what followeth.

My friend, you can't improve on that. If we just take that rule of John Wycliffe's and apply it to Hebrews, I don't think we will have trouble understanding this epistle. The phrase "partakers of the heavenly calling" would be perfectly meaningless apart from applying it to these Hebrew Christians.

"Consider the Apostle and High Priest of our profession, Christ Jesus." I would like to change the word *profession* to *confession*. And the word for "Christ" is not in the better manuscripts. Some of the newer translations have made that clear, and for that reason I would like to change the verse as follows: "Wherefore, holy brethren, partakers of the heavenly calling, consider the Apostle and High Priest of our confession [that which we confess], Jesus."

"Consider" Him. The Greek word translated by our English word *consider* conveys the fact of faithful attention, giving of time, and perceiving thoroughly with the mind. It is a very significant word, and we need to recognize that it means we are to give careful and serious and prolonged thought to this One.

"Consider the Apostle." What does the writer mean? The Lord Jesus was an apostle in the very basic meaning of the word. I don't think we need to read anything into this word. After all, what is an apostle? An apostle is one who is sent. Jesus was sent from God to this earth. "Consider the Apostle" because He was sent from God to this world. He is a messenger; He is God's messenger. He is the revelation of God. *Consider* Him. He comes from God as an Apostle, but notice also—

"Consider the Apostle and High Priest." His priestly function will be the subject of this epistle. (The writer just mentions it at this point, but when he comes back to it, that is all he is going to talk about. We will have to wait until we get to chapter 5 to see that.) A high priest is going in the opposite direction from an apostle. An apostle, like a prophet, came from God to man with a message; he spoke for God to man. However, a high priest was going on the other side of the freeway in the opposite direction. He was going from man to God; he represented man before God.

Now Jesus is our High Priest. Who is He? He is *Jesus*—the emphasis is upon His humanity. Again let me remind you that there is a Man in the glory today, and He represents us up there. My, I'm very happy that He is up there because we are told that He is an Advocate for us; He defends us; He is on our side.

There are times when I feel that I am not quite making myself clear when I am talking to somebody. For example, some time ago I tried to explain to an audience the feeling I had when I was told that I had cancer. I felt that I wasn't getting through, that they really didn't understand. But I have the comfort of knowing that there is somebody who understands—Jesus understands exactly how I felt.

The Lord Jesus Christ understands how you feel today. My friend, we need to consider this—give serious thought to it and our careful attention. We have an Apostle who came from God, and He is our High Priest who has gone back into God's presence and is there for you and for me today.

This is quite a wonderful verse, as you can see!

CHRIST IS SUPERIOR TO MOSES

Now the writer is going to show that Christ is superior to Moses. You see, having shown the superiority of Christ over the prophets who spoke for God in the Old Testament, and having shown His superiority over the angels, now he must show that He is superior to Moses because Moses is very important to the Hebrews. Several years ago a group of rabbis held a debate in Denver, Colorado. The subject of the debate was: "Who was greater, Abraham or Moses?" It is my understanding that it was decided that Moses was greater than Abraham. If that is true, if Jesus is to be considered, He has to be superior to Moses. The writer to the Hebrews is going to show this.

Who was faithful to him that appointed him, as also Moses was faithful in all his house [Heb. 3:2].

The Lord Jesus "was faithful to him that appointed him." He was faithful as He came down to this earth to represent God to man, and He is faithful as He represents us to God.

"Also Moses was faithful in all his house." Whose house are we talking about here? The word *house* occurs seven times in the next few verses. It is very important to determine whose house this is. Is it Moses' house? I don't think so. It is God's house. Moses was faithful in God's house. He was called to do a certain thing, and he did it. He was found faithful.

It is true that Moses made some mistakes—in fact, he recorded them. He wrote the Pentateuch, but the mistakes are not in what he wrote because God told him what to write. The mistakes were in his actions. He had a temper, and one time when God told him to speak to the rock, he hit it instead. It was wrong because that rock pictured Christ, and Christ's work for us. Many years earlier God had instructed Moses to smite the rock (see Exod. 17:6), and once smitten it need not be smitten again. Christ was smitten once for us; it was not necessary for Him to be smitten again. But Moses lost his temper. He did not know the implication of what he was doing when he smote the rock the second time. Although he made some mistakes, now that his life is past, it is wonderful indeed to note that the thing God remembers is his faithfulness. Faithfulness is the thing for which the Lord Jesus will commend His own—". . . Well done, thou good and faithful servant . . ." (Matt. 25:21). Regardless of who we are or what work the Lord has given us to do, we are to be faithful.

I once held meetings for a wonderful preacher. He did not play golf, but since his assistant did, his assistant took me out to play golf. While we were playing, he took the opportunity to let me know he was unfaithful to the pastor. He made little dirty digs about the man and said things he would not have said had he been faithful to the pastor for whom he was working. He was disloyal to him. The following day he said to me, "I have made arrangements for us to play at a certain golf course." I said, "I'm sorry, but I won't be able to go out today," and I never played golf with that man again.

The next time I went back to that church the assistant pastor was gone, and I asked the pastor about it. He told me, "That man got us in a lot of trouble. We found out he was very disloyal." I wondered at the time if I should have told the pastor about his assistant. I have no use for a man who is not faithful to the man he is to serve. If you cannot be faithful to the man you are working under, you ought to leave your position. If you are not faithful to him, you are not faithful to God. If you are like that, and I am especially thinking of pastors, then you are a man that cannot be trusted. I would never trust that man as an assistant pastor under any circumstances. That assistant pastor wrote to me later and wanted me to recommend him to a church. I did not recommend him. How can you recommend a man as a pastor when he was not faithful as an assistant?

God says that Moses was faithful. Wouldn't it be wonderful to hear God say of you, "He was faithful"?

Now notice that the verse began by saying that Christ was faithful—"who was faithful to him that appointed him." How then, was He superior to Moses?

> **For this man was counted worthy of more glory than Moses, inasmuch as he who hath builded the house hath more honour than the house [Heb. 3:3].**

Moses was faithful in God's house, but the Lord Jesus is the one who built the house. He is the Creator; Moses is a creature. There is the difference, my friend.

> **For every house is builded by some man; but he that built all things is God [Heb. 3:4].**

"Every house is builded by some man [someone]." You can't have a house without a builder—it can't just grow! Every house is built by someone.

"But he that built all things is God." The Lord Jesus is God, and He is the Creator. Moses never made that claim for himself.

> **And Moses verily was faithful in all his house, as a servant, for a testimony of those things which were to be spoken after;**

> **But Christ as a son over his own house; whose house are we, if we hold fast the confidence and the rejoicing of the hope firm unto the end [Heb. 3:5–6].**

Not only is Christ superior to Moses in that He is the Creator and Moses is a creature, but also the best thing that could be said of Moses is that he was a *servant* of God—never was he called a son of God. Christ is *the* Son of God. There is quite a difference between the son in the house and a servant in a house. So Christ is superior to Moses on two counts: Christ is the Creator and He is the Son. This is very important to see.

"If we hold fast the confidence and the rejoicing of the hope firm unto the end." Paul had a way of using "ifs," not as a condition but as a method of argument and of logic. We would understand him better if he had said, "*Since* we hold fast the confidence." In other words, if we are sons of God and if we are partakers of the heavenly calling, we *will* be faithful and we will hold fast. This is the proof that we are of God's house.

For example, 1 John 2:19 puts it this way, "They went out *from* us, but they were not *of* us; for if they had been *of* us, they would no doubt have continued with us: but they went out, that they might be made manifest that they were not all *of* us" (italics mine). I have always believed that God has permitted the cults to come along to draw out of the churches those who are not really believers. The cults serve as God's strainer. The proof that you are a child of God is that you hold to the faith. That doesn't *make* you a child of God, but it does prove that you *are* a child of God. If you are a believer, you will hold on, not because you are able but because *He* is able to make you stand.

So the writer of this Hebrew epistle (who I believe to be the apostle Paul) is using the "if" of argument. "If we hold fast the confidence and the rejoicing of the hope firm unto the end" means that you are a partaker of the heavenly calling; you are among the brethren.

I have always used the Bible as a means of testing. If a person really is a child of God, he will hold to the Word of God, and he is going to love the Word of God because he wants to hear his Father talking to him.

Now let's pursue a little further the contrast between Moses and the Lord Jesus Christ. Both Moses and the Lord Jesus enunciated an ethical system. It is generally agreed, even among those outside the fold of Christ, that Moses gave the greatest legal system which ever has been given and that Jesus in His Sermon on the Mount enunciated a tremendous system of laws. However, there is a vast difference between the two. You see, the laws which came from God through Moses had to do with *conduct*. However, when the Lord Jesus gave what we call the Sermon on the Mount (beginning with those marvelous beatitudes: "Blessed are the pure in heart, for they shall see God"), we see that instead of dealing with conduct, they deal with *character*. The ethical demands of Christ, apart from the saving grace of the Lord Jesus Christ in His death and resurrection, present a hopelessly high system. The Sermon on the Mount, apart from the redemption we have in Christ, has made more hypocrites in the church than anything else. Folk today teach the ethic and say we are to keep the commandments of the Sermon on the Mount! My friend, only through the redemption in Christ can we even *approach* that standard. When God spoke through Moses yonder on top of Mount Sinai, there was thunder and lightning and earthquake and terror. God warned the people to stand afar off and not to let even the cattle touch the mount. But in this age of grace God has not spoken in that manner; He has spoken from the top of a hill called Calvary. On that hill there was a cross and on that cross there was a broken, bruised, dying man—who was more than a man. He was God. And by His death upon that cross has flowed down to this world the *grace* of God.

How I thank God that He does not save by law! If He did, Vernon McGee would have to admit that he had failed and would have to look for another route. Thank God, there is another route—the *grace* of God.

"If [since] we hold fast the confidence and the rejoicing of the hope firm unto the end." Since you are a child of God, you will be *rejoicing* in the hope firm unto the end. This is another reason it is difficult to tell if folk in our churches are really saved. Some of them look and act as if they had been weaned on a dill pickle! They are not rejoicing in Christ.

Oh, my friend, Jesus is superior to the prophets. He is superior to angels, and He is superior to Moses. How wonderful He is! No wonder we are told to consider Him. In Hebrews 3:1 we are told to consider the Apostle and High Priest of our profession [confession], Christ. In Hebrews 12:3 we are going to be admonished again: "For consider him that endured such contradiction of sinners against himself, lest ye be wearied and faint in your minds." A person would be very discouraged if all he had was the Sermon on the Mount. I feel sorry for you if you are attempting to make the Sermon on the Mount your religion. If you don't have redemption in Christ, you are flying under false colors.

We are to consider Him—consider Him in His person, consider Him in His performance, His work upon the cross. Someone has put it poetically:

> When the storm is raging high,
> When the tempest rends the sky,
> When my eyes with tears are dim,
> Then, my soul, consider Him.

> When my plans are in the dust,
> When my dearest hopes are crushed,
> When is passed each foolish whim,
> Then, my soul, consider Him.

> When with dearest friends I part,
> When deep sorrow fills my heart,
> When pain racks each weary limb,
> Then, my soul, consider Him.

> When I track my weary way,
> When fresh trials come each day,
> When my faith and hope are dim,
> Then, my soul, consider Him.

> Clouds or sunshine, dark or bright,
> Evening shades or morning light,
> When my cup flows o'er the brim,
> Then, my soul, consider Him.
>   "Consider Him"
>   —Author Unknown

My friend, we are to consider Him in this epistle, and we will need the Spirit of God to make Him real to us.

THE PERIL OF DOUBTING

Wherefore (as the Holy Ghost saith, Today if ye will hear his voice [Heb. 3:7].

Notice that we have another *wherefore* which opens this section. We had a *wherefore* in verse 1, a *wherefore* here in verse 7, and we are going to have *wherefore* again in verse 10. It is a very important word. As I said, it is a swinging door that swings back into the past and swings out into the future. Also it is a danger signal as you come down the great highway that leads to heaven. In effect, it warns: Look both ways before you pull out—some crazy driver may be coming down the wrong side of the highway.

Wherefore, that is, in view of what has already been said, since the word spoken by the prophets and the word spoken by angels and the word spoken by Moses was so important, what about the importance of the word spoken by Jesus? We need to be very careful about doubting Him.

"Today if ye will hear his voice" begins the quotation from Psalm 95:7–11.

Harden not your hearts, as in the provocation, in the day of temptation in the wilderness:

When your fathers tempted me, proved me, and saw my works forty years.

Wherefore I was grieved with that generation, and said, They do alway err in their heart; and they have not known my ways.

So I sware in my wrath, They shall not enter into my rest.) [Heb. 3:8–11].

I believe that Christ is in every psalm, although I admit that I am not able to find Him in every psalm. However, here He is in Psalm 95: "For he is our God; and we are the people of his pasture, and the sheep of his hand. Today if ye will hear his voice, Harden not your heart, as in the provocation, and as in the day of temptation [testing] in the wilderness: When your fathers tempted [tested] me, proved me, and saw my work. Forty years long was I grieved with this generation, and said, It is a people that do err in their heart, and they have not known my ways: Unto whom I sware in my wrath that they should not enter into my rest" (Ps. 95:7–11).

Hebrews 3:7–11 interprets this portion of Psalm 95, and Israel is given to us as an example. Let's consider this for a moment. The generation of Israel that came out of Egypt doubted God, and because of their doubt they never entered the land of Canaan.

"They shall not enter into my rest." I have marked in my Bible that final word rest. There are at least a dozen references in this chapter and the next chapter to the word rest, but it does not always mean the same kind of rest.

There is the rest of salvation. The Lord Jesus referred to this in Matthew 11:28 when He said in effect, "Come unto me, all ye that labour and are heavy laden, and I will rest you; that is, I'll lift the burden of sin from you." Because He bore it for us upon the cross, our sins are forgiven, and we have redemption through His blood, even the forgiveness of sins. Therefore, you don't have to do anything so that God will forgive you; Christ has already done it when He died for you. All you have to do is believe and receive Christ.

The people of Israel now know the rest of redemption. They are no longer slaves in Egypt. They came out by blood—blood on the doorposts. They came out by power—God brought them across the Red Sea. God had delivered them. But then the Lord Jesus went on to say, "Take my yoke upon you, and learn of me; for I am meek and lowly in heart: and ye shall find rest unto your souls" (Matt. 11:29). That is a different kind of rest. It is not the rest of redemption; I would call it the rest of obedience, the rest of enjoying the Christian life.

When the children of Israel came out of the land of Egypt, as they crossed over the Red Sea, they sang the song of Moses—". . . I will sing unto the LORD, for he hath triumphed gloriously: the horse and his rider hath he thrown into the sea!" (Exod. 15:1). "God has delivered us—how great He is!" After they left Sinai, an eleven-day journey could have gotten them into the Promised Land. But no, they had to send spies in to search out the land. It wasn't necessary—God said He would take care of them, but they didn't believe God. So God yielded to their wishes and let them send in spies. Although the spies did see the wonderful land, they were most impressed by the giants, and they saw themselves as grasshoppers. They didn't see God. They returned to the people with a false report—except Caleb and Joshua who insisted that God could handle the giants if they trusted Him. But the people accepted the majority report (this is my reason for believing that committees are not satisfactory for doing the Lord's work), and they spent forty years on a journey that should have taken a few days. What was the reason? Unbelief.

You see, they didn't believe God enough to enter into the land. They believed Him enough to come out of Egypt, but not enough to enter Canaan. God said that that generation of unbelievers would die in the wilderness and He would bring their children into the Land of Promise. And we find later that Joshua did bring the next generation into the land. They had to cross another body of water, the river Jordan. How did they do it? Well, God sent the ark of the covenant (symbolic of God's presence) ahead on the shoulders of the priests. When their feet touched the brink of the river, the waters of Jordan were cut off. "And the priests that bare the ark of the covenant of the LORD stood firm on dry ground in the midst of Jordan, and all the Israelites passed over on dry ground, until all the people were passed clean over Jordan" (Josh. 3:17). Then they took twelve stones out of the middle of the river, where the priests still stood with the ark, and placed them as a memorial on the shore. Then they replaced them with twelve stones from the Land of Promise. When the waters of Jordan returned and covered those twelve stones, it was symbolic of the death of Christ. The twelve stones which were taken out of the river and placed as a monument on the other side speak of the resurrection of Christ.

Paul talks about this in Romans 6:4, where he says, "Therefore we are buried with him by baptism into death: that like as Christ was raised up from the dead by the glory of the Father, even so we also should walk in newness of life." We are now joined to a living Christ, and that is the only way we will enjoy Canaan. Canaan is not heaven. We are going to find out that there is an eternal rest, and Jesus gives that rest, but the question today is, "Have you entered into the rest that believers are to have as they sojourn on earth?" Are you a rejoicing Christian today? You will find out that the only way to do it is to study and believe the Word of God. How many Christians today, how many church members really study the Word of God? The Book of Hebrews is going to tell us that the Word of God is quick and powerful. Now that refers to the Lord Jesus Christ, but it also refers to the written Word. Therefore, the only way you and I can stay close to Him is to stay close to the Word of God. And the only way you and I can enjoy the grapes and fruits of the land, and the beauty and enjoyment of it, is by studying God's Word. Without a personal acquaintance with the Word of God, being a church member is like wearing a yoke, being browbeaten to give money, and having to do certain things. Everything is a duty instead of a drawing to the wonderful person of Christ.

The writer of this Hebrew epistle is speaking to those who are already saved but have not entered into the blessings of the Christian life. They doubt God, and as a result they are having a wilderness experience.

"Wherefore I was grieved with that generation, and said, They do alway err in their heart; and they have not known my ways." Notice where they erred. In their minds? No, in their hearts. Now hold that thought in your mind for a moment. The generation of Israel who came out of Egypt were cited to the Hebrew believers in the apostolic days as a warning not to repeat their sin. There was a danger of their doing that. And, my friend, we have the same danger, the danger of erring in our hearts.

"So I sware in my wrath"—it was not necessary for God to take an oath, but He did.

"They shall not enter into my rest." God said that, because of unbelief, the generation of Israelites would not enter into the land of promise. And, my friend, until you not only accept the Lord Jesus Christ as your Savior, but walk with Him by faith, committing your life to Him, you are not going to know anything about the joys of Canaan. Unfortunately, we have a great many wilderness Christians in our churches. The wilderness is a place of death; it is a place of unrest; it is a place of aimlessness; and it is a place of dissatisfaction. To those Israelites out there in the wilderness God said, "You are not going to know what rest is." And there are many believers today who just don't know what rest really means. They have never entered into it because they must enter by faith.

> **Take heed, brethren, lest there be in any of you an evil heart of unbelief, in departing from the living God [Heb. 3:12].**

You may ask, "Could that be true of a believer?" It certainly could. It is very important to realize that God was angry with their *sin*. What was their sin? It was not murder; it was not stealing; it was not lying. What was it? My friend, they didn't *believe* God. That was their great sin.

> **But exhort one another daily, while it is called Today; lest any of you be hardened through the deceitfulness of sin [Heb. 3:13].**

"Exhort one another"—we ought to do this, my friend, exhort and encourage one another.

"Lest any of you be hardened through the deceitfulness of sin." Although this is primarily a warning to believers not to miss their blessings because of the deceitfulness of sin, it has application to the unsaved person also. Unbelief in the heart is what is robbing folk of salvation. When someone tells me that he has an intellectual problem that hinders him from receiving Christ, I simply do not believe it.

Let me illustrate this from an experience I had when teaching a weekly Bible class in downtown Los Angeles. One evening a broker noticed the great crowd going into the church. They all had Bibles, and they looked as if they were interested in where they were going, so he was curious as to what could attract so many people to church in the middle of the week. Now this broker was a fine man in many ways.

If you had met him, you would have said he was a fine man. Well, he followed the crowd into church and stayed through the service. Later he came up to me and said, "All you did was teach the Bible! Is that what brings people in?" I told him that I thought it was since that's all we did on Thursday nights. Well, the man continued to come on Thursday nights, and then he started coming on Sundays, and soon he was under conviction.

One day he came to my study and said, "I thought I was a Christian. Now I know I am not. I am only a member of a church. But, I have a few intellectual problems with some of the things you have said. One of them is the story of Jonah. It is impossible for me to believe that a man could live inside a fish for three days and nights."

I asked him, "Who told you that Jonah lived three days and three nights inside a fish?"

"I have heard preachers say it. Isn't it in the Bible?"

"Not in my Bible." So I turned to the Book of Jonah and showed him what it did say, then turned to the New Testament and read what Jesus had said about it: "For as Jonas was three days and three nights in the whale's belly; so shall the Son of man be three days and three nights in the heart of the earth" (Matt. 12:40). I said to this broker, "If you are going to have trouble with the resurrection of Jonah, then you will have trouble with the resurrection of Jesus."

"Well," he said, "I didn't know it was that way. That is no problem for me at all now."

"Do you have another intellectual problem?"

"Maybe I don't."

I looked him straight in the eye and asked. "What sin do you have in your life that is keeping you from Christ?"

He turned red and asked, "Has somebody been telling you about me?"

"No, I just know that your intellectual problem is really a heart problem. There is something in your life that is keeping you from Christ."

He broke down. In fact, he wept and confessed that he had been paying the rent for his secretary's apartment and was spending a great deal of time there. I asked if his wife knew about it. He said that he had kept it a secret. Then I asked him, "Then that's your trouble, isn't it—you wouldn't want to give up your secretary for Christ?"

He looked at me and said, "Yes." Then he said, "I'll stop the rent and I'll talk to her tomorrow."

Well, he not only talked to her, but he fired her. She threatened to expose him, but she didn't. He got down on his knees that very day in my office and accepted Christ as his Savior.

My friend, I have been a preacher for a long time, and I have learned that people don't really have intellectual problems which keep them from Christ, but they sure do have sin problems.

There is another passage of Scripture (in 2 Corinthians 3, beginning with verse 6) that deals with Moses, which I would like to call to your attention. "Who also hath made us able ministers of the new testament [covenant]; not of the letter, but of the spirit: for the letter killeth, but the spirit giveth life." The Law condemns us, you know, but only the Holy Spirit can give us life. "But if the ministration of death, written and engraven in stones [this is the Ten Commandments], was glorious, so that the children of Israel could not stedfastly behold the face of Moses for the glory of his countenance; which glory was to be done away." Paul is not saying that the Law wasn't glorious; it *was*, but that glory was to disappear. Now let's drop down to verse 11: "For if that which is done away was glorious, much more that which remaineth is glorious." He is making a contrast between the glory of the Law, which actually made Moses' face shine, and the greater glory that we have in Christ. "Seeing then that we have such hope, we use great plainness of speech: And not as Moses, which put a veil over his face, that the children of Israel could not stedfastly look to the end of that which is abolished" (2 Cor. 3:12–13). You see, Moses didn't put a veil over his face as a dimmer, to dim the glory (which is the general interpretation), but the glory was disappearing and he put a veil over his face so that folk wouldn't know about its disappearance. But there is another glory now, the glory which is in Christ. "But their minds were blinded: for until this day remaineth the same veil untaken away in the reading of the old testament; which veil is done away in Christ. But even unto this day, when Moses is read, the veil is upon their heart"

(2 Cor. 3:14–15). You see, unbelief is not an intellectual problem; it is a heart problem. Perhaps you, my friend, are one who has not come to Christ because there is sin in your life and you do not want to give it up. The minute your heart is ready to give it up, at that moment your "intellectual" problems will dissolve. He will take the veil away from your mind, and you can come to Christ and be saved. Now notice verse 16: "Nevertheless when it [the heart] shall turn to the Lord, the veil shall be taken away." The veil will be removed from your mind when your heart turns to Christ. And the next verse: "Now the Lord is that Spirit: and where the Spirit of the Lord is, there is liberty." The Holy Spirit will move into your life and make Christ real to you, as He is doing for multitudes of folk in our day. Then when we come to Him—". . . we all, with open face beholding as in a glass the glory of the Lord, are changed into the same image from glory to glory, even as by the Spirit of the Lord" (2 Cor. 3:17–18). If you turn to Him—oh, my friend, the future that will await you as you grow in grace and in the knowledge of Him!

Now let's return to verse 13 where we are reminded, "But exhort one another daily, while it is called Today; lest any of you be hardened through the deceitfulness of sin." We as believers need to beware of the deceitfulness of sin. We can actually come to the place where we feel our lives are *satisfactory* to God although we are leading a wilderness life. For example, a believer can be dishonest and yet say that his conscience does not condemn him! Then he should condemn his conscience because it has become hardened through continuance in sin. I know men in the ministry who have been totally dishonest; they have been found to be liars, yet they can get down on their knees and pray the most pious prayers I've ever heard. And their conscience does not condemn them. Of course it doesn't condemn them because it has become hardened; they are permitting sin in their lives.

This writer of the Hebrew epistle goes back to the wilderness experience of Israel, applies it to the Hebrew believers of the first century, and steps on our toes also. It is the Holy Spirit who applies these truths to our own hearts.

**For we are made partakers of Christ, if we hold the be-
ginning of our confidence stedfast unto the end [Heb.
3:14].**

"We are made partakers of Christ." Just think of that! We are *in* Christ.
He *belongs* to us.

"If we hold the beginning of our confidence stedfast unto the end"
is the same argument he used in verse 6. We prove that we are members of Christ's house, that we belong to Him, "if we hold fast the confidence and the rejoicing of the hope firm unto the end."

Now in this section the emphasis is upon the *rest* which is ours if
we trust Christ. Scripture presents a fivefold rest: (1) creation rest; (2)
entrance into Canaan; (3) the rest of salvation; (4) the rest of consecra-
tion; and (5) heaven. Here the writer is talking about the rest of fully
trusting God, not only for salvation but for daily living.

**While it is said, Today if ye will hear his voice, harden
not your hearts, as in the provocation [Heb. 3:15].**

The quotation concludes with a quotation from Psalm 95, which we
have already seen in verses 7 and 8. Obviously he repeats it to remind
the reader that these truths are not for yesterday only, but for us today.

If you would ask me, "Preacher, what is the great sin in your life,
what is it that has held you back more than anything else?", I would
have to admit that it is *unbelief.* As I look back upon my years of ministry, I realize that I did not believe God as I should have. And today
there is one thing I want above everything else, and that is to *believe*
God. I want to commit my life to Him completely, turn everything over
to Him.

Flying from London to Los Angeles not long ago, we had a cloud
cover until we got over Greenland. Then I could see the icebergs. They
may be pretty in pictures, but when I looked at them from a height of
thirty-eight thousand feet, they didn't look so pretty. They looked cold
and foreboding. I saw a glacier coming down between two mountains
to the water's edge. I prayed right there. I said, "Lord, You know I trust
You when I am on the ground, but I have trouble trusting You when I

am flying. I am in a place right now where I need to trust You. Help me to put all of my weight down in Your arms and rest in You." For the first time in my life I went to sleep on an airplane! I have never done that before. I always had to stay awake so I could help the captain of the ship. But this time I went to sleep and left it all to the Captain of my salvation. When the plane landed in Los Angeles, I said, "Thank You, Lord, for the little victories. Maybe it wasn't much for You, but it was a whole lot for me."

My friend, this is the "rest" the writer of this Hebrew epistle is talking about, the rest of fully trusting God—not only for salvation but for daily living, for the help and the wisdom and the strength we need to live the Christian life.

The people of Israel wandered in the wilderness because they did not have faith to enter the Promised Land. As we have seen, Canaan does not represent heaven; it represents the place of spiritual blessing and victory. The apostle Paul was, I believe, speaking of his own experience when he cried, "O wretched man that I am! who shall deliver me from the body of this death?" (Rom. 7:24). That is not the cry of an unsaved man, it is the cry of a saved man who is a defeated Christian, who finds no satisfaction in Christ because he is not trusting. The problem was lack of faith.

For some, when they had heard, did provoke: howbeit not all that came out of Egypt by Moses [Heb. 3:16].

In the word *provoke* is the thought of God's being highly displeased with them because they had heard but did not believe. They had had faith enough to come out of Egypt, but that was as far as it went.

But with whom was he grieved forty years? was it not with them that had sinned, whose carcases fell in the wilderness? [Heb. 3:17].

Again, what was their sin that so grieved God? It was unbelief. We do not recognize—and I am sure they did not recognize—that doubting God's Word is such a serious sin. It is one of the worst because it leads

to other sins. For these Israelites in the wilderness it led to calf worship; it led to fornication; and it led to an absolute denial and rejection
of God as they turned their backs upon Him and even wanted to go
back to Egypt. They decided that slavery in Egypt was better than
walking by faith into the Promised Land!

Unfortunately, there are many Christians who still walk after the
world. They do not know what it is to really trust Christ and walk in
complete faith and trust in Him.

Now notice the question: "With whom was he grieved forty years?"
He was grieved with that crowd that came out of Egypt. They had
sinned, and their carcasses fell in the wilderness. Only two men out of
that crowd had faith to believe God, and they were Joshua and Caleb.
They were the only two who made it into the land. Even Moses did not
make it into the Promised Land, although his problem was not so
much a lack of faith as it was actual disobedience when he struck the
rock in anger rather than speaking to it as God had commanded.

And to whom sware he that they should not enter into his rest, but to them that believed not? [Heb. 3:18].

"And to whom sware he that they should not enter into his rest"—that
is, the rest of Canaan, he is not speaking of heaven. Because of their
unbelief they knew nothing about walking in Canaan, enjoying its
fruits, and finding satisfaction in simply trusting God. God said that
they would not enter into His rest. And He took an oath on that. Believe
me, God doesn't have to take an oath, but when He does, you know He
really means business.

Again, about whom is He talking? Those who did not believe.
Their worship of the calf and their fornication were not the sins that
kept them from God's blessing. It was the sin of *unbelief*. Oh, my
friend, unbelief not only robs us of blessing, but it leads to other sins as
well. The other day a man said to me, "Here I am a Christian and I did
this stupid thing." Well, the thing that he did was actually dishonest.
But the point is that he was deeply concerned about his dishonesty but
was ignoring the root of it—he hadn't believed God. That did not dis-
turb him at all.

So we see that they could not enter in because of unbelief [Heb. 3:19].

I suggest that you underline this verse in your Bible. This is what is robbing you and me of many blessings—*unbelief.*

CHAPTER 4

THEME: Christ is superior to Joshua; Christ is superior to the Levitical priesthood

In the first two verses of chapter 4 we have a continuation of the warning concerning doubting which was given in chapter 3.

Let us therefore fear, lest, a promise being left us of entering into his rest, any of you should seem to come short of it [Heb. 4:1].

We have come to the first "Let us" in this Epistle to the Hebrews. Constantly Paul urges the Hebrew believers to go on with the Lord; he is constantly challenging them. This is the first "Let us," but there is a whole lot of "Let us" in this epistle.

"Let us therefore fear." There are always those folk who are eager to find fault even with the Word of God, and they will say that this statement is a contradiction of other statements in the Bible. We are told in Romans 8:15, "For ye have not received the spirit of bondage again to fear. . . ." And in 2 Timothy 1:7 Paul wrote, "For God hath not given us the spirit of fear; but of power, and of love, and of a sound mind." Well, I have an answer for those folk in a message I have called, "When It Is Not Wrong to Fear." I hope that you are afraid of a rattlesnake. If I see one coming down the road, I don't simply move to the right-hand side, I give him the whole road! There are certain things that you and I would do well to fear—"Let us therefore *fear.*" I wish there were more concern among believers today about ignorance of the Word of God. In a church I pastored, a man was on our church board who was on about every board in town because he had a lot of money. He actually boasted of how many boards he was on. Then one day he boasted to me of how ignorant he was of the Word of God! The writer to the Hebrews said, "Let us therefore *fear.*" That man should have said to me with great concern, "Oh, my ignorance of the Word of God! I am afraid of it."

There are very few believers who are afraid of their ignorance of the Scriptures.

When Paul says, "Let us therefore fear," he is speaking of a good fear. When I take my grandsons for a walk, I warn them not to go out into the street. I want them to be afraid to go out into the street—that is a good fear. The Word of God says, "The fear of the LORD is the beginning of knowledge . . ." (Prov. 1:7). That is the kind of fear you and I are to have.

The fear he is talking about is for a purpose: "Lest, a promise being left us of entering into his rest, any of you should seem to come short of it." He is going to talk a great deal about rest in this chapter. The word rest occurs eight times here. There are several different kinds of rest, including Sabbath day or creation rest, and Canaan rest. Here he is speaking of Canaan rest. He is saying to believers, "Be afraid, because you do not want to miss it." How many believers are missing that rest today? Have you entered into rest? Do you know, Christian friend, what it is to really trust Christ and rest in Him?

> **For unto us was the gospel preached, as well as unto them: but the word preached did not profit them, not being mixed with faith in them that heard it [Heb. 4:2].**

Here is the "rest" of salvation, the rest of trusting Christ as Savior. They heard the Gospel but did not believe it.

CHRIST IS SUPERIOR TO JOSHUA

Moses led the children of Israel out of the land of Egypt, but he could not lead them into Canaan. Joshua led them into the land, but we will see here that he couldn't give them rest. Many of them never found rest—they never really laid hold of their possessions in the land. The world, the flesh, and the Devil rob many of the blessing God has for them. You and I live in a mean, wicked world. This world is not a friend of grace; it is not the friend of believers. Many of us have not discovered that yet.

> **For we which have believed do enter into rest, as he said, As I have sworn in my wrath, if they shall enter into my rest: although the works were finished from the foundation of the world [Heb. 4:3].**

He is discussing here salvation rest, the rest of trusting Christ. Let me ask you a question: If you knew a man who professed to be a Christian and whom you really believed was a born-again believer, and he suddenly stopped living the Christian life and began acting like the world, if he stopped going to church, stopped giving to the Lord's work, and stopped all his participation in Christian activity, would you think that he had lost his salvation? If you were that person, would you feel that you had lost your salvation? If you think that this would cause you to lose your salvation, may I say to you that way back in your mind and deep down in the recesses of your heart, you are not really trusting Christ. You are believing that those *activities* add to your salvation, but they do not. You are to completely trust Christ. Don't misunderstand me. I believe that if you are trusting Christ you are going to be doing those things, but doing those things has nothing in the world to do with your salvation. My friend, have you really entered into rest?

> **For he spake in a certain place of the seventh day on this wise, And God did rest the seventh day from all his works [Heb. 4:4].**

This is the Sabbath. God rested on the seventh day, and that was the Sabbath day. However, the Sabbath today is not a *day* you keep or observe. Have you entered into the *real* Sabbath today? Do you know what it is to trust Christ and Christ alone for your salvation? Are you trusting anything else? Is *He* it? Have you entered into rest?

I had a good friend who was a doctor and who observed Saturday as the Sabbath. We used to play tennis together, and we got pretty well acquainted with one another. One day after we had played three sets of tennis, we sat down on the bench, and we began to have what you would call a religious argument. He looked at me and said, "McGee, do you keep the Sabbath day?"

"Yes, I keep the Sabbath."

He looked at me real hard and said, "*What* day?"

I said to him, "Saturday, Sunday, Monday, Tuesday, Wednesday, Thursday, Friday, and then I start all over again on Saturday."

He said to me, "What in the world do you mean?"

"Well, the way I understand the Epistle to the Hebrews, the Sabbath day is now this day of grace in which we live, and Christ, after He died on the cross and came back to life, went back to the right hand of the Father and sat down. He sat down, not because He was tired, but because He had finished your redemption and mine. So now He tells me, 'You rest in Me.' I have a Sabbath day everyday—I rest in Christ."

That doctor friend looked at me in amazement. "Well, he said, "that's better than having just one day, isn't it?"

I said, "It sure is. Seven days a week is a sabbath of resting in Christ."

> **And in this place again, If they shall enter into my rest.**

> **Seeing therefore it remaineth that some must enter therein, and they to whom it was first preached entered not in because of unbelief [Heb. 4:5–6].**

It is unbelief that robs you of the rest of salvation, that robs you of the rest of satisfaction and blessing which God can give to you. Oh, the wonderful rest that He wants to give to us!

> **Again, he limiteth a certain day, saying in David, Today, after so long a time; as it is said, Today if ye will hear his voice, harden not your hearts [Heb. 4:7].**

He is not saying tomorrow, but today. *Today* is the day for you and me. Today, right now, wherever you are, look at your watch or clock. What time is it? Well, this is the time of salvation. *Now,* right now you can trust Christ to save you. "Today if ye will hear his voice, harden not your hearts."

> **For if Jesus had given them rest, then would he not afterward have spoken of another day [Heb. 4:8].**

Joshua is the Old Testament or Hebrew word for "savior"; *Jesus* is the Greek or New Testament word, meaning "savior." In the verse before us—Joshua: "For if Joshua had given them rest, then would he not afterward have spoken of another day." When Joshua was old and stricken in years, there was yet very much land to conquer. The people of Israel had not entered into all the blessing God had in store for them. But, my friend, if you trust Christ, Christ can let you enter into the Canaan of the present day, in which there will be fruit and blessing and joy in your life. Oh, how we need this today! What robs us of it? Unbelief.

> **There remaineth therefore a rest to the people of God [Heb. 4:9].**

Here the writer is projecting into the future when all the people of God are going to find a heavenly rest. Heaven will be a place of deep satisfaction, of real joy, and real blessing. "There remaineth therefore a rest to the people of God."

> **For he that is entered into his rest, he also hath ceased from his own works, as God did from his [Heb. 4:10].**

We shouldn't get the impression that when God rested on the seventh day He sat down and said, "My, I'm tired. I've been working for six days, eight hours a day, from sunup to sundown, and I'm weary! I'll pull up the rocking chair and rest." That is not the thought behind "rest" at all. The thought here is the rest of *completeness*. Creation is finished. God has never been in the business of creating since then. There were just so many atoms which He needed for His universe, and He just made them all at once. He hasn't made any more since then. Now there have been quite a few changes taking place in the universe, but it is just those original little atoms rearranging themselves.

You and I live in a universe where creation is over with—except in the new creation. That new creation began yonder at Calvary and the Day of Pentecost. "Therefore if any man be in Christ, he is a new creature: old things are passed away; behold, all things are become new"

(2 Cor. 5:17). Sons of God are the only things God is creating today—
through faith in Christ. And there is a rest that He has promised to
them. God has promised a heavenly rest, but, my friend, He wants us
to enjoy ourselves even *now*. As someone has said, "All the way to
heaven is heaven." We ought to enjoy this life. That is what the writer is
talking about here: God rested, He ceased from His labors, and He is
finished. Therefore, you do not have to lift your little finger to do something toward your salvation. Isn't it really a matter of conceit on our
part to think that you and I as sinners could do anything that would
cause God to say, "Oh my, what a nice little fellow you are! I'm so
happy to have you in heaven because you are going to add a great deal
to it."? Well, my friend, that is not the picture at all. He did it *all* for us.
Even our righteousness is filthy rags in His sight. He cannot accept our
righteousness because we really do not have any. "There is none righteous, no, not one" (Rom. 3:10). Therefore He offers a *finished* salvation to us, and when we trust Christ we become new creations in Him.

**Let us labour therefore to enter into that rest, lest any
man fall after the same example of unbelief [Heb. 4:11].**

I think the supreme satisfaction that can come to a child of God is that
he is in the will of God, doing the work of God, and trusting and just
resting in Him. That is the glorious place to which God wants you and
me to come. Mary came to that place. She sat at Jesus' feet while Martha was back yonder in the kitchen with those pots and pans. Martha
wanted to serve Christ, but she just didn't know what real rest was.
She probably decided she was going to bake something and reached
for a pan. It was not big enough and she was going to put it back and
get a bigger one, but she dropped it on the floor. What a time she had
with those pots and pans! She was really worn to a frazzle and finally
lost her temper. But Mary was just sitting at Jesus' feet, doing
nothing—she had already done her work. We need to learn to find our
satisfaction sitting at Jesus' feet.

"Let us labour therefore to enter into that rest." Someone will say,
"Do I have to *labor* to enter into rest?" Yes, my friend. This is sort of
like the Irishman who said he intended to have peace in his home even

if he had to fight for it. Fighting for peace? Yes! I wish America had learned that lesson. May I say to you, you must win a war before you can have peace. You have to have a victory before you can have peace. He says here, "Let us labor in order to rest." After all, when you have worked at something and come to the end of the day and sit down, isn't there a satisfaction in what you have done? Oh, today, we need to lay hold of God! To lay hold of God in prayer, and in faith, and to be used of Him. Oh, my Christian friend, let us *labor* toward that end.

"Lest any man fall after the same example of unbelief." The only thing in the world that can rob you of that rest is unbelief. Ever since I retired from the pastorate my prayer has been, "Oh, God, help me to trust You." I was a pastor for forty years, and very frankly, I look back and have to say that I wish I had trusted Him more. Many times I was so fearful and unbelieving. So today I want to simply lean back and trust Him. How wonderful He is! He is worthy of our trust.

> **For the word of God is quick, and powerful, and sharper than any twoedged sword, piercing even to the dividing asunder of soul and spirit, and of the joints and marrow, and is a discerner of the thoughts and intents of the heart [Heb. 4:12].**

"For"—Paul used the words *wherefore, therefore,* and *for* as cement to hold together his argument. Someone has said, "Regardless of what you want to say about Paul, one thing you have to say is that Paul is logical." Paul was a marvelous logician, and I believe he wrote this epistle. *For* is a little word, but it is a big word. Someone has said, "God swings big doors on little hinges." Here is one of those little hinges, but there is a big door hanging on it.

"The word of God." There are some expositors who consider the "word" here not to be the written Word, but the living Word who is the Lord Jesus Christ. However, in Scripture the written Word is called the living Word. I believe the reference here is primarily to the written Word of God. As the written Word reveals Christ—it is a frame that reveals the living Christ—the reference here could be to both the written and living Word.

Quick is "living." The Word of God is living.

"Powerful"—the Greek word is *energes*, meaning "energizing." The Word of God is living, and it energizes.

"Sharper than any twoedged sword." I had a professor in seminary who said to a group of us young preachers: "Remember when you preach the Word of God that it is quick and sharp, but it is a *twoedged* sword. It will cut toward the congregation, but the other side is going to cut toward you. Therefore, don't preach anything that you are not preaching to yourself." I have found many times in my ministry that I am preaching to myself. The sermon might not have been for anybody else, but it *was* for me.

I have a friend who likes to kid me about my recording of tapes for our radio Bible study broadcasts. He says, "There you are, sitting in your study, just talking to yourself!" Very candidly, that is the way it works out many times as I sit there teaching the Bible. I'm speaking to myself. It may not apply to anyone in the radio audience, but it applies to me. The Word of God is twoedged. It will cut toward the other fellow, but it will also cut toward you and me. The Word of God is a twoedged sword, and it will penetrate.

Paul wrote to the Thessalonians, "For this cause also thank we God without ceasing, because, when ye received the word of God which ye heard of us, ye received it not as the word of men, but as it is in truth, the word of God, which effectually worketh also in you that believe" (1 Thess. 2:13). The Thessalonians received the Word not just as an ordinary word, but they received it as the very Word of God. Paul said that when he gave out the Word of God ". . . my speech and my preaching was not with enticing words of man's wisdom, but in demonstration of the Spirit and of power" (1 Cor. 2:4). We receive many letters from those who listen to our radio Bible study broadcasts, from folk who through the Word have been brought to a saving knowledge of Christ, brought to a place where they enjoy their Christian faith, and brought to a place where they enjoy prayer. That is the purpose of the Word of God—it will have an effect upon you and your life.

It has been said, "The Word of God will keep you from sin, or sin will keep you from the Word of God." A great many believers do not spend enough time in the Word of God. A great many preachers do not spend enough time in the Word of God. The greatest discipline a preacher can have is to go through the Bible book by book with his congregation. That is a discipline which even if it does not help the congregation, it will surely help the preacher. In every church which I have served as a pastor, I have gone through the Bible with the congregation. It surely helped me—it was good for me. The Word of God is sharp; it is living and powerful and sharp.

"Piercing even to the dividing asunder of soul and spirit." There are many people who try to make a distinction between soul and spirit, devising some ingenious psychological division between the two. Do you know that only the Word of God can divide the soul and spirit? You and I cannot do that. When I talk about the soulish part of man and how God has given us the Holy Spirit, I suddenly find that I am no longer making a distinction between the soul and spirit—only the Word of God can do that. There are times in the Scriptures when "soul" and "spirit" are used synonymously. There are other passages where it is clear that the soul and spirit are separate and are not the same thing. Only the Word of God can divide soul and spirit.

"Of the joints and marrow." The Word can get right down even in this flesh of ours and make a distinction (see Ps. 32:3).

"A discerner of the thoughts and intents of the heart." The Greek word for "discerner" actually means "critic." We have today many critics of the Word of God. However, the Word of God is the critic. It criticizes you. It criticizes me. No man is in a position to sit in judgment on the Word of God. There are many reasons for that, and one reason is that there is no other book like it. The Word of God was written over a period of fifteen hundred years, by about forty-five different authors, some of whom had never heard of the others. Yet they are all in agreement. They all present a glorious salvation. May I say to you, no man is in a position to sit in judgment on such a remarkable book.

I had an opportunity one time to listen to a very fine, brilliant, Shakespearean scholar. Many scholars are not humble, but this man was a very humble man. When he had finished his lecture he said, "Today I have attempted to give to you a critique of Shakespeare, but now I would like to say to you that I am in no position to sit in judgment on Shakespeare." It took a humble man to say that. Nor can any man sit in judgment on the Bible, my friend. You really don't know enough to sit in judgment on this Book. This Book surely sits in judgment on us. It is sin that keeps men from Christ today. It is not intellectual problems of the head, but it is problems in the heart which keep men from God.

"A discerner [critic] of the *thoughts* and *intents* of the heart." You see, the Bible does not deal with *acts* primarily. What the hand does is because of what the heart thought. The heart had the action of the hand in hand before the hand got hold of it. Therefore the Word of God goes down and deals with the heart. The Lord Jesus said, "For out of the heart proceed evil thoughts, murders, adulteries, fornications, thefts, false witness, blasphemies" (Matt. 15:19). My, that's a filthy list, but that is what is in your heart and mine. "The heart is deceitful above all things, and desperately wicked: who can know it?" (Jer. 17:9). No man can, but God does. The Word of God gets down and deals with the nitty-gritty of our hearts. It gets down and meets us right where the rubber meets the road, right down where you and I live and move and have our being.

> **Neither is there any creature that is not manifest in his sight: but all things are naked and opened unto the eyes of him with whom we have to do [Heb. 4:13].**

You cannot conceal anything from God. I labored under the delusion as a young Christian that I would not let God in on everything in my life, even my plans. I prayed that He would give me certain things and do certain things for me, but I never let Him know my motives. I thought the prayer would sound better that way. To tell the truth, I didn't need to let Him know my motive because He knew it all the time. He is the one who knows the thoughts of the heart, and everything is open to Him. My friend, your life is an open book to Him. People ask me, "Do you think we ought to confess everything to Him?" Well, why not? He already knows—you might just as well tell Him all about it.

CHRIST IS SUPERIOR TO THE LEVITICAL PRIESTHOOD

Beginning with verse 14 of this chapter through verse 28 of chapter 7, the writer of this epistle is going to show that Christ is superior to the Levitical priesthood. This was very important for Hebrew believers to see because they were accustomed to approaching God through their high priest of the Levitical order, the priests who served first in the tabernacle and then in the temple. It was through them that they made their commitment to God and brought their sacrifices.

OUR GREAT HIGH PRIEST

The Lord Jesus Christ himself is our Great High Priest. Paul was so concerned and enthusiastic about the priesthood of Christ that way back in chapter 3 he said, "Wherefore, holy brethren, partakers of the heavenly calling, consider the Apostle and High Priest of our profession, Christ Jesus" (Heb. 3:1). He wanted to get the folk who were reading the epistle to immediately consider our High Priest. This is going to be the subject of much of the rest of the epistle, and, of course, there will be application of this great truth also.

> **Seeing then that we have a great high priest, that is passed into the heavens, Jesus the Son of God, let us hold fast our profession [Heb. 4:14].**

Christ is our High Priest. The pagan notion of priesthood colors our thinking in reference to a priest. A pagan priest actually barred the approach to God, claiming possession of some mystical power essential to bringing an individual to God. A person had to go through this priest who claimed to have this particular access. That type of thing denies the finished work of Christ and the priesthood of all believers. The priesthood of all believers was one of the great truths which John Calvin emphasized. All of us need a priest—we have a lack; we need help, and we all have our hang-ups. Job's heart-cry was, "Neither is there any days man betwixt us, that might lay his hand upon us both" (Job 9:33). Job longed for a mediator or priest who would stand between him and God, who would put one hand in Job's hand and his other hand in God's hand, and thus bring them together. Christ is that mediator, that priest, through whom every believer has personal access to God.

"We have a high priest, that is passed into the heavens." Let me say right away that the Lord Jesus Christ was not a priest while here on the earth. The only mention in Scripture of His ever making any kind of sacrifice (He never needed to make a sacrifice for Himself, of course) was the time He told Simon Peter to catch a fish and take the gold piece out of its mouth that He might pay a necessary temple tax from which the priests were exempt. He did that, I think, to make it very clear that He was not a priest here on earth. To be a priest you had to be born in the line of Aaron, of the tribe of Levi. The Lord Jesus was a member of the tribe of Judah. He was not in the priestly line. He was in the kingly line. When He was here on earth He came as a prophet speaking for God. He went back to heaven a priest to represent us to God. He became a priest when He ascended into heaven. He died down here to save us, and He lives up there to keep us saved. It is true that when He was here He offered Himself upon the cross, and that is the function of a priest, but to be a priest to represent you and me He had to wait until He returned to heaven.

Christ occupies a threefold office: (1) He was a prophet when He came over nineteen hundred years ago—that is the past; (2) He is a priest today—that is for the present; and (3) He is coming someday to rule as a king—that is for the future. He occupies all three of these offices, and He is the great subject of this Epistle to the Hebrews.

"Let us hold fast our profession"—"profession" should be confession. Paul says, "Let us," to challenge us, to call us to do it, actually, to command us to do it. Let us hold fast our confession.

Notice that he does not say, "Let us hold fast our salvation." He is not talking about our salvation, but about our testimony, our witness down here. He is talking about our living for Christ. Christ died down here to save us, and He lives up yonder to keep us saved and to enable us to give a good witness. Some people say, "I can't live the Christian life." Well, I have news for you. It is true that you cannot live the Christian life, and God never asked you to live the Christian life. I have been thankful that He has not asked that of me because I have tried it, and it didn't work. We cannot do it in our own strength, but He asks that He might live it through us. He lives up yonder in order that you and I might hold fast to our confession, our testimony down here.

When we come to chapter 11 we will find a regular roll call of the heroes of the faith which shows what faith has done in the lives of men and women in all ages. All of those listed there had a good witness, a good report. Theirs was a good witness through faith—they lived by faith.

For we have not an high priest which cannot be touched with the feeling of our infirmities; but was in all points tempted like as we are, yet without sin [Heb. 4:15].

You will notice in your Bible that the word yet is in italics, meaning that it has been added by the translators. Christ was tempted without sin—tested without sin. In the testing of Jesus in the wilderness, He could not have fallen because He is the God-man. However, the pressure of testing was actually greater upon Him than it would be upon us. He could say, ". . . the prince of this world cometh, and hath nothing in me" (John 14:30). Satan finds something in me and in you also, but he could find nothing in the Lord Jesus. Let me illustrate this for you: A boat standing in water can only tolerate so much pressure. If the pressure becomes too great, there will be a rip in the hull of the boat and water will come in, and thus the pressure is removed. That is the way you and I are—we give in to the pressure, we yield, and then the pressure is gone. Jesus never did yield, and therefore there was a building up of pressure that you and I never experience. In the same way, the cars of a freight train all have a weight limit which they can carry. If that limit is exceeded, you will have a swaybacked car, one that is bowed down in the middle. It gives in—it can only carry so heavy a load. That is true of all of us. We can carry just so much and not any more. May I say to you, the weight of temptation Jesus Christ could carry was infinite—He was tested without sin. But He was tested, and for that reason He knows how we feel. We have a High Priest who understands us.

I have always felt that for the nation Israel the death of Aaron was in one sense of greater significance than the death of Moses. Aaron was their great high priest. Many Israelites had been brought up with Aaron, had played with him as a boy, and had gone through the wilderness with him. They could go to Aaron and say, "Look, Aaron, I did this, and I should not have done it. I have brought my sacrifice." And Aaron could sympathize with them. He knew exactly how they felt. But when Aaron died I imagine they wondered whether that new priest, the son of Aaron, would understand. Would he be able to sympathize and to help? We have a Great High Priest who is always available, and He does understand. He does not understand us theoretically, but down here He was tested, and He was "touched with the feeling of our infirmities." He knew what it was to hunger. He knew what it was to be touched with sorrow—Jesus wept! He was "touched with the feeling of our infirmities . . . yet without sin."

> **Let us therefore come boldly unto the throne of grace,**
> **that we may obtain mercy, and find grace to help in time**
> **of need [Heb. 4:16].**

"Let us therefore come boldly unto the throne of grace." I must confess that I have never really liked our translation of "boldly," but neither do I know how to change it. The word *boldly* has the thought of being brazen—there is sort of a flippancy suggested by it—or of being cocksure. That is really not the idea. It is a very interesting word in the Greek—*parrhesia*. It denotes the freedom of speech which the Athenians prized so highly. They were perhaps the first to feel that the average citizen should have freedom to speak.

"Let us therefore come [with great freedom] unto the throne of grace." We can speak freely to the Lord Jesus Christ. I can tell Him things that I cannot tell you. He understands me. He knows my weaknesses, and I might just as well tell Him. I have learned to be very frank with Him. I have not attempted to become buddy-buddy with Him—I despise that approach. He is *God*, and I come to Him in worship and with reverence. But I am free to speak because He is also a man. He is God, but He is a man, and I can come to Him with great freedom. I can tell Him what is on my heart. I can open my heart to Him. I suspect, therefore, that all these very pious and flowery prayers we make are not impressive to Him—especially when we are attempting to cover up what is in our hearts and lives. I wonder if the Lord doesn't tune us out when we do not come to Him with freedom and open our hearts to Him. That is one of the reasons our prayer meetings are not more effective. We come to Him rather restrained, without being open and sincere.

"Unto the throne of grace." God's throne is a throne of grace. Formerly a throne of judgment, it is now a mercy seat, a throne of grace.

"That we may obtain mercy." We need a lot of mercy. Mercy is something that is in one sense negative—it speaks of the past. We are redeemed by the mercy of God. "Not by works of righteousness which we have done, but according to his mercy he saved us . . ." (Titus 3:5). He has been merciful to me.

"And find grace to help in time of need." Help is a very positive thing—it speaks of the future. We may obtain mercy and find grace to help in time of need. David wrote, "The LORD is my shepherd; I shall not want (Ps. 23:1). I have noticed that one of the newer translations reads, "The LORD is my shepherd; I *have not* wanted." How ridiculous! Of course, he had not wanted in the past, but the beauty of it is that David could say, "I *shall* not want." Why? Because the Lord is my Shepherd. I have an High Priest up yonder, and I can go to Him as my shepherd.

By the way, have you been to Him yet today? What did you tell Him? Did you tell Him that you love Him? Did you confess your sins to Him? Well, why don't you? He already knows it, but why don't you tell Him? Don't put up a front to Him. He aleady knows that you can come to Him only on His merit. Go to Him with freedom and *talk* to Him—there is mercy and grace to help in time of need.

CHAPTER 5

THEME: Definition of a priest

This chapter continues the great theme of Christ as our High Priest, showing that He is superior to the Levitical priesthood, with which the Hebrews were so familiar.

In the first ten verses we have the definition of a priest. Christ, as we have already said, has the threefold office of prophet, priest, and king. He is God's final word to man. In Christ God has said all He intends to say. As a prophet, He spoke over nineteen hundred years ago. Now He is the Word of God. He is the priest for the now generation. Some day in the future He is going to come as king. Right now He is our Great High Priest. We have access to Him. He is a Great High Priest, just as Aaron was a great high priest.

And every believer is a priest, just as all the tribe of Levi were priests. We can offer sacrifices to God as priests. Praise is a sacrifice that we can offer. Have you praised Him today? We can also offer our substance, the fruit of our hands, the fruit of our minds, or our time. Believers can make all of these things an offering to Him. And prayer is the work of a priest. To recognize our position and privilege eliminates all of the mechanics we have today. It puts aside all of the methods that we use. We see two extreme approaches to God through worship today. One is a very emotional approach, and the other is a very ritualistic approach. Both of them are soulish and not spiritual worship at all. We simply need to come to Him and get rid of all the mechanics and the methods.

Someone sent me a story about the astronaut who was in his capsule just ready to close the door in preparation for the launching, when a reporter asked him a question. Reporters, I have observed, sometimes ask some rather asinine questions. This reporter asked, "How do you feel when you are an astronaut ready to take off?" The astronaut replied, "How would you feel if you were sitting on top of fifty thousand parts, each supplied by the lowest bidder?" That is the way many people worship today. They are ritualistic or they are emotional; they go by their feelings rather than by the Word of God.

The concluding verse of chapter 4 urges us to come in freedom to the throne of grace. We need mercy and we need help. He is in the position to supply these because He is our Great High Priest.

DEFINITION OF A PRIEST

For every high priest taken from among men is ordained for men in things pertaining to God, that he may offer both gifts and sacrifices for sins [Heb. 5:1].

This verse gives us the definition of a priest. He must be taken from among men, which means he must be a *man*. He must be a representative, you see. He represents man, but he represents man to God. He is ordained *for* man in things pertaining to God. Because he goes before God, he must be acceptable to God. That is the suggestion in "is ordained for men in things . . . to God." In verse 4 we are told specifically that no man takes this honor unto himself, but he that is called of God, as was Aaron. He must be ordained of God. Therefore a priest is: (1) taken from among men; (2) ordained for men (on behalf of men); and (3) goes to God for men.

We can now draw a distinction between a priest and a prophet. A priest goes from man to God; he represents man before God. A prophet comes from God to man with a message from God. Therefore the Old Testament priest did not tell men what God had to say—that was the ministry of the prophet. The priest's ministry was to represent man before God. Now in the present age our Lord Jesus Christ is the only priest. It is He who represents us before God.

The priesthood functions, not for lost sinners, but for saved sinners. You will recall that John said, "My little children [my little born ones], these things write I unto you, that ye sin not . . ." (1 John 2:1). Well, I'm sorry, John, but you are talking to a boy who has sinned. Even as a child of God I have sinned. I am thankful that he covered me when he added, "And if any man sin, we have an advocate with the Father, Jesus Christ the righteous." Christ represents me up there.

When my enemy, Satan, accuses me before the Father, the Lord Jesus Christ represents me. He is my High Priest. That is one reason why I would never be satisfied just to have a priest on earth. I want to make this very clear, and I am not attempting to be critical. If someone is going to represent me before God, I want to be sure that he is acceptable to God. Is he one who has accreditation? Has he passed his bar examination so he can represent me in heaven? We can pray for one another, but we cannot represent one another in heaven. But because I need somebody to represent me, I am very happy that I have my Great High Priest who represents me before the Father.

"That he may offer both gifts and sacrifices." Notice that the priest may offer both gifts and sacrifices. The writer is going to make it abundantly clear that He had something to offer: He offered Himself. Compared to the precious blood of Christ which has redeemed us, silver and gold would be like lead or dirt.

"That he may offer both gifts and sacrifices for *sins*"—notice that it is sins, not sin; it is plural. It speaks of the life of the believer. For example, when you lost your temper, did you go to God and confess that sin? You have a representative who is there to make intercession for you. He represents you before God.

> **Who can have compassion on the ignorant, and on them that are out of the way; for that he himself also is compassed with infirmity [Heb. 5:2].**

We have a Great High Priest who could say, when He came to the end of His ministry on earth, "Which of you convinceth [convicts] me of sin? . . ." (John 8:46). The Lord's disciples had been with Him for three years, and if there had been anything wrong, they would have known. He was impeccable; He did not commit any sin. Yet because He lived on this earth as a man, He understands us.

He "can have compassion on the ignorant." What does that mean? "Compassion on the ignorant" refers to sins of ignorance. Leviticus 4:1–2 deals with these sins. If you don't think you have committed a sin in the past few days, and you feel like you have really been living in the heights, I have news for you. You commit sins that you are not even aware of, and He, our Great High Priest, takes care of that for us. He can have compassion on the ignorant. You see, "There is a way which *seemeth* right unto a man, but the end thereof are the ways of death" (Prov. 14:12, italics mine). "All we like sheep have gone astray . . ." (Isa. 53:6). God compares us to sheep because all sheep go astray.

"He Himself also is compassed with infirmity." Aaron was touched with infirmity or weakness, but Christ was touched with a *feeling* of our infirmity or weakness. He knows how we feel about things. He is the perfect mediator, you see. When we fall, He doesn't get down in the dirt with us; He is there to lift us out of it.

The trouble with Aaron was that he might condone the sins that he also had committed. Or he might condemn the sins that he had not committed himself. That would always be a danger. But Christ is able to show mercy, and He neither condones nor condemns. When we come to Him to make confession of our sins, He doesn't give us a little lecture about doing better next time. He just extends mercy to us. "If we confess our sins, he is faithful and just [as our High Priest] to forgive us our sins, and to cleanse us from all unrighteousness" (1 John 1:9). It is wonderful to have a High Priest like He is!

Now we see a contrast between Aaron and Christ because there is no counterpart of this requirement of the Aaronic priesthood in our Lord Jesus Christ.

And by reason hereof he ought, as for the people, so also for himself, to offer for sins [Heb. 5:3].

You will recall that on the great Day of Atonement Aaron first brought a sacrifice and took the blood into the Holy of Holies for his own sins. He had to have his own sin question settled first before he could represent the people. There is no counterpart of this in Christ. Christ did not have to make an offering for Himself. He made an offering for you and me.

And no man taketh this honour unto himself, but he that is called of God, as was Aaron [Heb. 5:4].

As we saw earlier, Christ was a priest because He was acceptable to God.

So also Christ glorified not himself to be made an high priest; but he that said unto him, Thou art my Son, to-day have I begotten thee [Heb. 5:5].

I want to make it abundantly clear that the "begotten" here has nothing to do with the birth of Christ in Bethlehem. It has everything to do with the garden near Calvary where He was buried after His crucifixion because that is where His resurrection took place. He was begotten from the dead. His priesthood began when he went back to heaven, and that speaks of His resurrection.

As he saith also in another place, Thou art a priest for ever after the order of Melchisedec [Heb. 5:6].

The order of Aaron is not adequate to set before us the priesthood of Christ. So our Lord is not an High Priest in the order of Aaron, although Aaron is the type, and Christ the antitype. Christ is the Son, and Aaron is just a servant.

"Thou art a priest for ever after the order of Melchisedec." Who is Melchisedec (spelled Melchizedek in the Old Testament)? The only historical record that we have of him is in Genesis 14 where he is described as a "priest of the most high God." He went out to congratulate Abraham on his victory over Chedorlaomer and his allies in which Abraham recovered all of the citizens of Sodom and Gomorrah, including his nephew Lot, and also brought back all the booty. The king of Sodom met Abraham and offered him all of the booty. Abraham was under some temptation, but he turned down the offer. In Genesis 14:18 we read, "And Melchizedek king of Salem brought forth bread and wine: and he was the priest of the most high God." The account continues in Genesis 14:19-20, "And he blessed him, and said, Blessed be Abram of the most high God, possessor of heaven and earth: And blessed be the most high God, which hath delivered thine enemies into thy hand. And he gave him tithes of all." We are told that Melchizedek was the king of Salem (*Salem* means "peace") and he was also king of righteousness. He walks out onto the pages of Scripture out of nowhere—we have no inkling where he came from—and he walks off the page of Scripture the same way. There is no other historical mention of him.

In Psalm 110 we see the prophecy of Melchizedek—that there is coming one who is to be a priest after the order of Melchizedek. Hebrews now gives us the interpretation of Melchizedek.

Let me say at this point that there are some very fine expositors who think that Melchizedek is the preincarnate Christ. Well, I cannot accept that interpretation because Melchizedek is a *type*, of the Lord Jesus. Obviously, the antitype cannot be the type—or you wouldn't have a type. Therefore, I interpret Melchizedek as a human being who was the literal king of Salem. Two excellent expositors, G. Campbell Morgan and Lewis Sperry Chafer, hold that he was the preincarnate Christ; so you will be in good company if you take that position.

However, I believe Melchizedek was a type given to us by Moses and guarded by God. He just walks out of nowhere and walks back into nowhere. He had no beginning or ending of days. The Lord Jesus Christ is the beginning and the end. He is Alpha and Omega (see Rev. 1:8). He started it all, and He will end it all. He is the AMEN. He is the One who is the *eternal* God and as such has no beginning or ending. The writer is telling us that we have a priest like that—He is after the order of Melchizedek. We will see an interpretation of this in chapter 7.

This brings us to a verse that I feel totally inadequate to deal with. I feel that I am just standing on the fringe in my understanding of it.

Speaking of the Lord Jesus—

> **Who in the days of his flesh, when he had offered up prayers and supplications with strong crying and tears unto him that was able to save him from death, and was heard in that he feared [Heb. 5:7].**

Scripture tells us that on three occasions Jesus wept. I am of the opinion there were other occasions, but the record gives us only three. One was at the tomb of Lazarus. At that time, although He knew He would restore Lazarus to life, His heart went out in sympathy to the two sisters who were so deeply grieved. Because He wept for *them*, I know how He feels when you and *I* stand at the graveside of a loved one.

At another time He wept over the city of Jerusalem. Since He wept over Jerusalem at that time, I am sure He has wept many times over the cities in which you and I live. They certainly provide Him with reasons for weeping!

Then the third time He wept was in the Garden of Gethsemane. Why did He weep there? A cynic and unbeliever made the statement that he wished he had been present so he could have killed the Lord Jesus in some way other than by crucifixion. In saying this, it is evident that he perceived something that some believers do not firmly grasp. He would have liked to have kept Jesus from the Cross, which is exactly what the Devil wanted to do. I believe that Satan attempted to slay the Lord Jesus in the Garden of Gethsemane. When He prayed in the garden, "Let this cup pass from me" (see Luke 22:42), the "cup" was death. He did not want to die in the Garden of Gethsemane.

"And was heard in that he feared." If our Lord Jesus prayed in the garden to let the cup pass because He didn't want to die on the cross, then He wasn't heard—because He *did* die on the cross. My friend, He was heard; He did not die in the Garden of Gethsemane.

You see, prophecy had made it abundantly clear that He was to die on a cross. We do not have a better picture of crucifixion than in Psalm 22. The cross was an altar on which the Son of God shed His blood, paying the penalty for your sin and my sin. "The life of the flesh is in the blood," God said, "and I have given it to you upon the altar to make an atonement for your souls . . ." (Lev. 17:11). In the Old Testament the blood of animal sacrifices only covered over the sin, but the blood of Christ was given "to make atonement for your souls." Christ shed His blood on the cross, which was an altar. He told Nicodemus, "And as Moses lifted up the serpent in the wilderness, even so must the Son of man be lifted up" (John 3:14). He did not want to die in the garden. That, I think, was His prayer, His human prayer, as He wept and sweat great drops of blood. Our Lord was near death as He approached the cross, and He prayed to be delivered from death so that He could reach the cross. And we are told that He "was heard in that he feared."

"In that he feared"—fear is not something that is always wrong, as we have seen elsewhere in this epistle. It would be abnormal not to fear some things. And I think we need a little more fear in our churches; we need the fear of the Lord, which is the beginning of wisdom. The Lord Jesus *feared*.

> **Though he were a Son, yet learned he obedience by the things which he suffered;**
>
> **And being made perfect, he became the author of eternal salvation unto all them that obey him [Heb. 5:8–9].**

"And being made perfect"—that is, made complete, made full.

"Eternal salvation"—the only kind of salvation He offers is eternal. If you can lose it tomorrow, then, my friend, it is not eternal. It is some other kind of salvation. But He offers only *eternal* salvation.

"Unto all them that obey him." What is obedience? A crowd of people asked Jesus, ". . . What shall we do, that we might work the works of God?" (John 6:28). Jesus replied, ". . . This is the work of God, that ye believe on him whom he hath sent" (John 6:29). Do you want to obey God? Then *trust* Christ. That is what He is saying.

But there is something here that I do not understand—I am frank to admit it. "Though he were a Son, yet learned he obedience by the things which he suffered." Why did the Son of God need to learn obedience by suffering? And why did He need to be made perfect when He already was perfect? I stand here in the presence of a mystery, a mystery that I cannot fathom. I know only that God got something out of the death of Christ that has made heaven more wonderful and has added something to heaven where everything is perfection and that the Son of God has learned something!

Now I am well acquainted with the explanation that men gave, but none of them satisfy me. I just recognize that it is a great mystery. Christ took upon Himself our humanity, and in that humanity He obeyed God. He said, "I have come to do my Father's will" (see John 6:39). Paul said of Him, ". . . [He] took upon him the form of a servant, and was made in the likeness of men: And being found in fashion as a man, he humbled himself, and became *obedient* unto death, even the death of the cross" (Phil. 2:7–8, italics mine). My friend, I want you to know that when I die (if the Lord tarries) I won't do it obediently. I don't want to die. I think it is morbid when folk always talk to me about wanting to die. I want to live on earth as long as I can. When I had cancer, many people wrote to me and said, "We are praying for you. We are asking that the Lord spare your life." I am thankful because the Lord heard those prayers. But one dear lady in Southern California wrote to me and said, "I am not praying that the Lord will leave you here. I know you are ready to go, so I am praying that He will take you home." I wrote back to her in a hurry and said, "Listen, you let the Lord alone in this matter. It is just between Him and me. I don't want you to tell the Lord when you think He ought to take me home. I want to stay here, and I'll appreciate it if you don't pray that prayer any more. At least, change it. Tell the Lord that you made a mistake, and that McGee wants to stay."

When the writer to the Hebrews says that Christ learned *obedience* by the things which he suffered, I don't understand it. I simply recognize that I am in the presence of a mystery—that even my Lord *learned* something!

> **Called of God an high priest after the order of Melchisedec [Heb. 5:10].**

Called means "saluted" and refers to Melchizedek.

Now the writer will discuss this matter of the priesthood of Christ, that Melchizedek was given to us in the Old Testamant as a type of the high priesthood of our Lord Jesus Christ.

THE PERIL OF DULL HEARING

The writer puts up the third danger signal; it is like a red light flashing. He is getting ready to bring us out on the highway, but before he does, we've got to look both ways. There is the danger of being dull of hearing. He devotes the remainder of the chapter to this because in the next chapter (after still another danger signal) he will deal with the great subject of Christ our High Priest after the order of Melchizedek.

Of whom we have many things to say, and hard to be uttered, seeing ye are dull of hearing [Heb. 5:11].

"Of whom we have many things to say." The writer says, "I still have a lot of things to say."

"And hard to be uttered." Why is it hard to be uttered?

"Seeing ye are dull of hearing." The writer, who I think was Paul, could state it all right, but they couldn't grasp it.

Have you ever said to your husband or wife after a Bible-teaching sermon, "I don't think the pastor was quite up to it today. I didn't feel his message was equal to what he is capable of giving."? Did you ever stop to think that the problem that day may have been with you? Are you dull of hearing? The problem may not be in the speaking, but the problem may be in the hearing.

Ear trouble, today, is the big problem of believers. Christ as a priest after the order of Melchizedek is a difficult subject, and the writer is going to deal with it forthrightly. To understand the subject requires sharp spiritual perception. It requires folk to be spiritually alert and to have a knowledge of the Word of God and to be *close* to it. The Hebrew believers who are being addressed here had a low SQ, not an IQ, but an SQ—spiritual quotient. It was hard to teach them because it was difficult to make them undersatnd. They were babies, as many of the saints are today, and they want baby talk even from the preacher. They don't want to hear anything that is difficult to understand. This is the reason some preachers are getting by with murder in the pulpit—they murder the Word of God. They absolutely kill it and substitute something from their own viewpoint, and the congregations like that kind of baby talk.

For when for the time ye ought to be teachers, ye have need that one teach you again which be the first principles of the oracles of God; and are become such as have need of milk, and not of strong meat [Heb. 5:12].

"Ye have need that one teach you again which be the first principles of the oracles of God." Some of them want a D.D. degree, but they don't even know their ABCs. "First principles" is from the Greek word *stoicheion* (from which we get our English word *atom*, by the way), meaning "primary elements"—the ABCs of the Christian life. They ought to be teachers and mature saints, but instead they are still little babies needing someone to burp them.

For example, one Sunday after the morning service a church member stopped to talk to me while I was shaking hands with folk who were leaving. He said, "Dr. McGee, do you have anything against me?" I said, "No. Why do you say that?" "Well, you passed me yesterday on the street, and you didn't speak to me." That is baby talk. I didn't even see that person, and it is perfect nonsense to talk like that. Someone else said, "Why didn't the soloist sing this morning? We wanted to hear the soloist sing." Oh, my gracious, what little babies, wanting their rattles, and wanting the bottle with the nipple on it!

To these Hebrew believers the writer says, "You are such as have need of milk, and not of strong meat. You are not of age; you are not full grown; you haven't reached maturation." Now a baby cannot eat meat, but an adult can enjoy milk. I will admit that a lot of saints today sit and listen to baby talk from the pulpit. It is tragic indeed that they have to endure this, but they do.

For every one that useth milk is unskilful in the word of righteousness: for he is a babe [Heb. 5:13].

He doesn't know the Word of God.

I don't want to step on your toes, my friend, but I'd love to be helpful to you. You cannot grow apart from the Word of God. I don't care how active you are in the church. You may be an officer. You may be on every committee in the church. You may be a leading deacon or elder. I don't care who you are, or what you are; if you are not studying the Word of God, and if you don't know how to handle it, you are a little baby. It is tragic to occupy a church office when you are just a little baby. You ought to come on and grow up. It is tragic that there are

people who have been members of the church and have been saved for
years, and they are still going around saying, "Goo, goo, goo." They
have nothing to contribute but little baby talk. All they want is to be
burped periodically.

> **But strong meat belongeth to them that are of full age,
> even those who by reason of use have their senses exer-
> cised to discern both good and evil [Heb. 5:14].**

In 1 Corinthians 3:1–2, Paul says, "And I, brethren, could not speak
unto you as unto spiritual, but as unto carnal, even as unto babes in
Christ. I have fed you with milk, and not with meat: for hitherto ye
were not able to bear it, neither yet now are ye able." In 1 Peter 2:1–2,
Peter says, "Wherefore laying aside all malice, and all guile, and hy-
pocrisies, and envies, and all evil speakings, As newborn babes, desire the sincere milk of the word, that ye may grow thereby."

CHAPTER 6

THEME: Danger signal: peril of departing

This chapter, by all odds, contains the most difficult passage in the Bible for an interpreter to handle, regardless of his theological position. Dr. R. W. Dale, one of the great minds in the earlier field of conservative scholarship, wrote:

> I know how this passage has made the heart of many a good man tremble. It rises up in the New Testament with a gloomy grandeur, stern, portentous, awful, sublime as Mount Sinai when the Lord descended upon it in fire, and threatening storm clouds were around Him, and thunderings and lightnings and unearthly voices told that He was there.

Every reverent person has come to this section with awe and wonder. And every sincere expositor has come to this passage with a sense of inadequacy, and certainly that is the way I approach it.

DANGER SIGNAL: PERIL OF DEPARTING

In the previous chapter the danger signal was the peril of dull hearing. Now as the Hebrew Christians can already see persecution coming, there is a danger of their turning from their confession of Christ and going back to Judaism. He mentions the baby things of Judaism which had to do with ritual. He encourages them to grow up, to go on to maturity.

> **Therefore leaving the principles of the doctrine of Christ, let us go on unto perfection; not laying again the foundation of repentance from dead works, and of faith toward God [Heb. 6:1].**

"Leaving the principles of the doctrine of Christ" is literally "leaving the word of the beginning concerning Christ." For a builder it means to leave the foundation and go up with the scaffolding, or for a child in school to go on from his ABCs to work on his B.A. or Ph.D. It is preparing believers for a trip up to the throne of God.

"Let us go on" is horizontal, not perpendicular.

"Unto perfection" is maturity, full age.

There are six foundational facts in the Old Testament which prefigure Christ in ritual, symbol, and ceremony: (1) repentance from dead works; (2) faith toward God; (3) doctrine of baptisms; (4) laying on of hands; (5) resurrection of the dead; and (6) eternal judgment.

"Repentance from dead works." The works were the works of the Mosaic Law. They were continually trying to keep the Law, then breaking it, then repenting. That is baby stuff, the writer tells them.

"And of faith toward God." The Old Testament taught faith toward God; so just to say you believe in God doesn't mean you have come very far. The Old Testament ritual presented a faith in God by approaching Him through the temple sacrifices, not through Christ as High Priest.

Of the doctrine of baptisms, and of laying on of hands, and of resurrection of the dead, and of eternal judgment [Heb. 6:2].

"Doctrine of baptisms [washings]" has nothing to do with New Testament baptism. They refer to the washings of the Old Testament ritual, and there were many of them. The Hebrew believers were wanting to return to these things which were only shadows; they were the negatives from which the spiritual pictures were developed. They prefigured Christ, the reality.

"Laying on of hands." This was also an Old Testament ritual. When a man brought an animal offering, he laid his hands on its head to signify his identification with it. The animal was taking his place on the altar of sacrifice.

"Resurrection of the dead" was taught in the Old Testament, but now they needed to come up to the resurrection of Christ and to the living Christ.

"Eternal judgment" was taught in the Old Testament.

And this will we do, if God permit [Heb. 6:3].

This brings us to that passage which has caused as many difficulties as any in the Scriptures. Some consider it the most difficult passage to interpret.

> **For it is impossible for those who were once enlightened, and have tasted of the heavenly gift, and were made partakers of the Holy Ghost,**

> **And have tasted the good word of God, and the powers of the world to come,**

> **If they shall fall away, to renew them again unto repentance; seeing they crucify to themselves the Son of God afresh, and put him to an open shame.**

> **For the earth which drinketh in the rain that cometh oft upon it, and bringeth forth herbs meet for them by whom it is dressed, receiveth blessing from God:**

> **But that which beareth thorns and briers is rejected, and is nigh unto cursing; whose end is to be burned.**

> **But, beloved, we are persuaded better things of you, and things that accompany salvation, though we thus speak [Heb. 6:4–9].**

Verse 9 is the key to the passage, but we need the context to understand what is being said.

As we study this section, we are immediately confronted with the amazing fact that generally commentators have avoided this chapter. Even such a man as Dr. G. Campbell Morgan, the prince of expositors, has completely bypassed it in his book on Hebrews. However, when we do come upon the interpretations available and summarize each, we can well understand why men have chosen to remain clear of this scene of confusion because we can get many interpretations.

In the interest of an honest search after the evident meaning of these verses, let us examine some of the interpretations.

The most unsatisfactory to me of all interpretations is that the Christians mentioned here are Christians who have lost their salvation. That is, they were once saved but have lost their salvation. There are many folk who hold this position, and for the most part they are real born-again Christians themselves. However, this belief makes them as uncomfortable as I am when I am making a trip by plane. I know that I am just as safe on that plane as anyone there, but I do not enjoy it as some of them do. There are many folk today who are not sure about their salvation and therefore are not enjoying it. Nevertheless they are saved if they have fixed their trust in Christ as their Savior. The essential thing is not the amount of faith they have but the one to whom it is directed. They turn to this passage of Scripture more than any other since they deny that we have a sure salvation which cannot be lost and that the believer is safe in Christ.

I want to make it abundantly clear that I believe we have a sure salvation because Scripture is very emphatic on this point. Paul says in Romans 8:1: "There is therefore now no condemnation to them that are in Christ Jesus . . ." and, my friend, he expands that great truth to the triumphant climax of such a bold statement as, "Who shall lay any thing to the charge of God's elect? It is God that justifieth" (Rom. 8:33). The throne of God is back of the weakest, humblest man who has come to trust Christ, and today there is not a created intelligence in God's universe that can bring a charge against one of these who is justified through faith in His blood. Paul continues in Romans 8:34–39: "Who is he that condemneth? [1] It is Christ that died, [2] yea rather, that is risen again, [3] who is even at the right hand of God, [4] who also maketh intercession for us." My friend, if you drink in those words you will have a great foundation of assurance. "Who shall separate us from the love of Christ? shall tribulation, or distress, or persecution, or famine, or nakedness, or peril, or sword? As it is written, For thy sake we are killed all the day long; we are accounted as sheep for the slaughter. Nay, in all these things we are more than conquerors through him that loved us." Does that satisfy you? Well, let's keep going. Paul is not through yet. "For I am persuaded, that neither death, nor life, nor angels, nor principalities, nor powers, nor things present, nor things to come, nor height, nor depth, nor any other creature, shall be able to separate us from the love of God, which is in Christ Jesus our Lord." Can you mention anything that Paul didn't mention in this passage? Can you find anything that could separate you from the love of Christ? May I say to you, this list takes in the whole kit and caboodle. Here we have a guarantee that *nothing* can separate us from the love of God—nothing that is seen, nothing that is unseen, nothing that is natural, nothing that is supernatural can separate us from the love of God which is in Christ Jesus our Lord.

The Lord Jesus Christ also makes some tremendous statements about our absolute security. Listen to Him, trust in Him, and believe Him. The Word of God is living and powerful, my friend. Jesus said, "My sheep hear my voice, and I know them, and they follow me: And I give unto them eternal life" (John 10:27–28). What kind of life? *Eternal* life. If you can lose it, it is not eternal! "And they shall never perish, neither shall any man pluck them out of my hand. My Father, which gave them me, is greater than all; and no man is able to pluck them out of my Father's hand" (John 10:28–29). It is not a question of your ability to hold on to Him; it is His ability to hold on to you. He says here with the infinite wisdom and full authority of the Godhead that He *can* hold us and that they who trust Him shall never perish. The question is: Is your hope fixed in God who is all-powerful, or in a god who may suffer defeat?

I have cited only some of the passages of Scripture that make it abundantly clear that you and I cannot be lost after we have been born again into the family of God. We become children of God through faith in Christ. Once a person has become a child of God through faith in Christ he has *eternal* life. I cannot accept the interpretation that the people in Hebrews 6:4–9 were once saved and had lost their salvation.

There is a second interpretation that has some merit in it. There are those who contend that this is a hypothetical case. "*If* they shall fall away." There is only a possibility that this might happen. The writer does not say that it happens, only that it might be possible. Those who contend that this is the correct interpretation say that it is the biggest "IF" in the Bible, and I would agree with them. If I did not take another position on the intrepretation of this passage in Hebrews, I would accept this one.

The third interpretation points out that in verse 6 there really is no "if" in the Greek. It is a participle and should be translated "having fallen away." Therefore these folk have another interpretation, which is that the passage speaks of mere professors, that they are not genuine believers. They only profess to be Christians. Well, I cannot accept this view, although such scholars as Matthew Henry, F. W. Grant, and J. N. Darby hold this thinking, as does C. I. Scofield in his excellent reference Bible—a Bible which I feel every Christian should own, although in some cases I do not concur with the interpretations given in the notes, as in the instance before us.

I do not accept the view that these folk are professors rather than genuine believers. The Bible does speak of those who merely profess Christ. There are apostates in the church. For instance Peter in his second epistle wrote: "It has happened unto them according to the true proverb, The dog is turned to his own vomit again; and the sow that was washed to her wallowing in the mire" (2 Pet. 2:22, ASV). Those folk were professors, not genuine believers. But in chapter 6 we find genuine believers because they are identified as such in many ways. If you will move back into chapter 4 to get the entire passage, you will notice that it is said of these people that they are dull of hearing (see Heb. 5:11)—it does not say that they are dead in trespasses and sins (see Eph. 2:1). And in Hebrews 5:12 it says that "when for the time ye ought to be teachers, ye have need that one teach you . . . and are become such as have need of milk. . . ." They need to have milk because they are babes. An unsaved person doesn't need milk; he needs *life*. He needs to be born again. He is dead in trespasses and sins. After he is born again, a little milk will help him. Therefore I believe the writer to the Hebrews is addressing baby Christians, and he is urging them to go on to maturity.

There are other expositors who take the position that since the ones spoken of here are Jewish believers of the first century, the warning can apply only to them. At the time Hebrews was written, the temple was still standing, and the writer is warning Jewish Christians about returning to the sacrificial system because in so doing, they would be admitting that Jesus did not die for their sins. Therefore, those who hold this reasoning say that verses 4–6 apply only to the Jewish Christians of that day and have no reference to anyone in our day.

There is still another group which stresses the word *impossible* in Hebrews 6:4. It is impossible to renew them—the thought being that it is impossible for man, but it is not impossible with God. They remind us that the Lord Jesus said that ". . . It is easier for a camel to go through the eye of a needle, than for a rich man to enter into the kingdom of God" (Matt. 19:24). Of course it is impossible for any of us to enter heaven on our own; we must have a Savior, a Redeemer. Therefore, this again is an interpretation that I cannot accept.

You can see that there are many interpretations of this passage—and, of course, there are others which I have not mentioned.

Now there is one interpretation that has been a real blessing to my heart, and I trust you will follow me patiently, thoughtfully, and without bias as we look at it. Because I was dissatisfied with all the interpretations I had heard, I actually felt sad about it. Then several years ago I picked up a copy of *Bibliotheca Sacra*, a publication of the Dallas Theological Seminary, and read an article on the sixth chapter of Hebrews written by Dr. J. B. Rowell, who was then pastor of the Central Baptist Church in Victoria, British Columbia. His interpretation was the best that I had heard. I give him full credit for it. This is not something that I thought of, although I have developed it to fit my own understanding, of course.

First of all, let me call to your attention that the writer is not discussing the question of salvation at all in this passage. I believe he is describing saved people—they have been enlightened, they have tasted of the heavenly gift, they have been made partakers of the Holy Spirit, and they have tasted the good Word of God and the powers of the world to come.

The whole tenor of the text reveals that he is speaking of *rewards* which are the result of salvation. In verse 6 he says, "If they shall fall away, to renew them again unto repentance"—not to salvation, but to *repentance.* Repentance is something that God has asked *believers* to do. For example, read the seven letters to the seven churches in Asia, as recorded in Revelation 2 and 3. He says to every one of the churches to repent. That is His message for believers.

So the writer of Hebrews is talking about the *fruit* of salvation, not about the *root* of salvation. Notice verse 9 again: "But, beloved, we are persuaded better things of you, and things that *accompany* salvation [he hasn't been discussing salvation but the things that accompany salvation], though we thus speak." He is speaking of the fruit of the Christian's life and the reward that comes to him as the result. The whole tenor of this passage is that he is warning them of the possibility of losing their reward. There is danger, Paul said, of our entire works being burned up so that we will have nothing for which we could be rewarded. "For other foundation can no man lay than that is laid, which is Jesus Christ. Now if any man build upon this foundation gold, silver, precious stones, wood, hay, stubble; Every man's work shall be made manifest: for the day shall declare it, because it shall be revealed by fire; and the fire shall try every man's work of what sort it is. If any man's work abide which he hath built thereupon, he shall receive a reward. If any man's work shall be burned, he shall suffer loss: but he himself shall be saved; yet so as by fire" (1 Cor. 3:11–15). The work of every believer, my friend, is going to be tested by fire, and fire *burns!* The work you are doing today for Christ is going to be tested by fire. For example, when all of those reports that some of us preachers have handed in about how many converts we have made are tried by fire, they will make a roaring fire—if our work has been done in the flesh rather than in the power of the Spirit. We will have nothing but wood, hay, and stubble that will all go up in smoke.

Someday every believer is going to stand before the judgment seat of Christ. I wish I could lay upon the heart of believers that it is not going to be a sweet little experience where the Lord Jesus is going to pat us on the back and say, "You nice little Sunday school boy, you didn't miss a Sunday for ten years. You are so wonderful." The Lord is going to go deeper than that. He is going to test you and see if you really had any fruit in your life. Have you grown in grace and knowledge of Him? Have you been a witness for Him? Has your life counted

for Him? Have you been a blessing to others? My Christian friend, I am
not sure that I am looking forward to the judgment seat of Christ because He is going to take Vernon McGee apart there. I will not be
judged for salvation, but because I am saved, He is going to find out
whether or not I am to receive a reward.

Now notice that he is illustrating the fruit of the Christian's life:
"For the earth which drinketh in the rain that cometh oft upon it, and
bringeth forth herbs meet for them by whom it is dressed, receiveth
blessing from God: But that which beareth thorns and briers is rejected, and is nigh unto cursing; whose end is to be burned" (vv. 7–8).
If the believer's life brings forth fruit, it receives blessing from God; if
it brings forth thorns and briers, it is rejected.

When the apostle Paul wrote to Titus, a young preacher, he dealt
with the matter of works: "Not by works done in righteousness, which
we did ourselves, but according to his mercy he saved us . . ." (Titus
3:5, ASV). From this, one might be inclined to think that Paul is not
going to have much regard for good works, but move down in that
same chapter to verse 8: ". . . I desire that thou affirm confidently, to the
end that they who have believed God may be careful to maintain good
works. . . ." Good works do not enter into the matter of salvation, but
when one becomes a child of God through faith in Christ, works assume supreme importance. My friend, if you are a Christian, it is important that you live the Christian life.

When I was a university student the psychologists were discussing
a matter which they have moved away from now. It was: Which is more
important, heredity or environment? Well, my psychology professor
had a stimulating answer. He said that before you are born, heredity is
more important, but after you are born, environment is the major consideration! Now let's carry that line of thought over to our present
study. Before you are born again, works do not enter in because you
cannot bring them to God—He won't accept them. Scripture says that
the righteousness of man is filthy rags in His sight (see Isa. 64:6). You
don't expect God to accept a pile of dirty laundry, do you? He is accepting sinners, but He accepts us on the basis of the redemption that
we have in Christ. When we receive Christ as Savior, we are born anew
and become a child of God. When that happens, we are, as Peter put it,

". . . an elect race, a royal priesthood, a holy nation, a people for God's own possession, that ye may show forth the excellencies of him who called you out of darkness into his marvellous light" (1 Pet. 2:9, ASV). Now after you have been saved, you are to show forth by your good works before the world that you are redeemed to God. Therefore the Christian has *something* to show forth, and that is the thing which is to be judged. If he is going to continue as a baby and be nothing but a troublemaker, turning people from Christ instead of to Christ, there will certainly be no reward. In fact, there will be shame at His appearing.

"For as touching those who were once enlightened and tasted of the heavenly gift, and were made partakers of the Holy Spirit, and tasted the good word of God, and the powers of the age to come, and then fell away, it is impossible to renew them again unto repentance; seeing they crucify to themselves the Son of God afresh, and put him to an open shame" (vv. 4–6, ASV). These verses bring us to the very center of this study.

"And then fell away"—*fell away* is an interesting word in the Greek. It is *parapitō* and means simply "to stumble, to fall down." It would be impossible to give it the meaning of "apostatize." It is the same word used of our Lord when He went into the Garden of Gethsemane, *fell* on His face, and prayed.

There are many examples in Scripture of men who "fell away." The apostle Peter fell, but he was not lost. The Lord Jesus said to him, "I have prayed that your faith might not fail" (see Luke 22:32). Peter suffered loss, but he was not lost. John Mark is another example. He failed so miserably on the first missionary journey that when his uncle Barnabas suggested that he go on the second journey, Paul turned him down. He as much as said, "Never. This boy has failed, and as far as I am concerned, I am through with him" (see Acts 15:37–39). Well, thank God, although he stumbled and fell, *God* was not through with him. Even the apostle Paul, before he died, acknowledged that he had made a misjudgment of John Mark. In his last epistle he wrote, ". . . Take Mark and bring him with thee; for he is useful to me for ministering" (2 Tim. 4:11). Now, neither Peter nor John Mark lost their salvation, but they certainly failed and they suffered loss for it.

Read again verse 1 and notice that the writer is talking to folk about repentance from dead works—not salvation, but *repentance*. You will recall that John the Baptist also preached this to the people: "Bring forth therefore fruits worthy of repentance . . ." (Luke 3:8). He was referring to that which is the *evidence* of repentance. Repentance in our day does not mean the shedding of a few tears; it means turning right-about-face toward Jesus Christ, which means a change of direction in your life, in your way of living.

Many of the Jewish believers were returning to the temple sacrifice at that time, and the writer to the Hebrews was warning them of the danger of that. Before Christ came, every sacrifice was a picture of Him and pointed to His coming, but after Christ came and died on the cross, that which God had commanded in the Old Testament actually became *sin*.

You see, those folk were at a strategic point in history. The day before the crucifixion of Jesus they had gone to the temple with sacrifices in obedience to God's command, but now it was wrong for them to do it. Why? Because Jesus had become that sacrifice—once and for all. Today if you were to offer a bloody sacrifice, you would be sacrificing afresh the Lord Jesus because you would be implying that when He died nineteen hundred years ago it was of no avail—that you still need a sacrifice to take care of your sin. It would mean that you would not have faith in His atonement, in His death, in His redemption. As someone has said, we either crucify or crown the Lord Jesus by our lives. Today we either exhibit a life of faith or a life by which we crucify Him afresh—especially when we feel that we have to get back under the Mosaic system and keep the Law in order to be saved. It is a serious matter to go back to a legal system.

Notice again verse 6 as the Authorized Version translates it: "If they shall fall away, to renew them again unto repentance." Actually the *if* is not in the text at all. It is "having fallen away," or "then fell away"—a genitive absolute. It is all right to use the "if," providing you use it as an argument rather than in the sense of a condition.

Why would it be impossible to renew them again unto repentance? Remember we are talking about the fruit of salvation. It is a serious thing to have accepted Christ as Savior and then to live in sin, to nullify what you do by being a spiritual baby, never growing up, doing nothing in the world but building a big pile of wood, hay, and stubble. Paul said the same thing in different language in 1 Corinthians 3:11 which says, "For other foundation can no man lay than that is laid, which is Jesus Christ." Your salvation is a foundation. You rest upon it, but you also build upon it. You can build with six different kinds of materials—wood, hay, stubble, gold, silver, and precious stones. What kind of building materials are you using today? Are you building up a lot of wood, hay, and stubble? There is a lot of church work today that is nothing but that. We are great on organizations and committees, but do our lives really count for God? Are there going to be people in heaven who will be able to point to you and say, "I am here because of your life and testimony," or "I am here because you gave me the Word of God." Oh, let's guard against building with wood, hay, or stubble!

By the way, there is a difference between a straw stack and a diamond ring. And you can lose a diamond ring in a hay stack because the ring is so small. I am afraid that a great many folk are building a straw stack to make an impression. One pastor told me, "I'm killing myself. I have to turn in a better report this year than the report last year. We have to increase church membership and converts and giving to missions." Oh, if this pastor would only dig into the Scriptures and spend much time in God's presence. Then he would be teaching his people the Word and many would be turning to Christ and would be growing in their relationship with Him. Every man's works are going to be tested by fire. What will fire do to wood, hay, and stubble? Poof! It will go up in smoke. There will be nothing left. That is what the writer is saying.

In John 15 the Lord Jesus talks about the fact that He is the vine, the genuine vine, and we are the branches. We are to bear fruit. "If ye abide in me, and my words abide in you, ye shall ask what ye will, and it shall be done unto you. Herein is my Father glorified, that ye bear much fruit . . ." (John 15:7–8). He wants us to bear much fruit. When there is a branch that won't bear fruit, what does He do? "If a man abide not in me, he is cast forth as a branch, and is withered; and men gather them, and cast them into the fire, and they are burned" (John

15:6). He will take it away; He will remove it from the place of fruit-bearing and that is what the Lord Jesus is saying.

I see God doing this very thing today. And as I look back over the years, I have seen many men work with wood, hay, or stubble. And I have seen others work with gold. I know a layman who was a very prominent Christian when I came to the Los Angeles area almost forty years ago. Then he became involved in a dishonest transaction. He has lost his testimony, and yet he was a very gifted and likeable man. I still consider him my friend, but I wouldn't want to go into the presence of Christ as this man will have to go when his life is over.

Also I recall a minister who was very attractive—a little too attractive. He was unfaithful to his wife, had an affair with another woman, and finally divorced his wife. And all the while he tried to keep on teaching! But his teaching didn't amount to anything—he was just putting up a whole lot of straw. He was not even baling hay; he was just making a big old haystack. Finally the match was put to it, I guess, because he certainly didn't leave anything down here.

Oh, how careful we should be about our Christian lives. And we cannot live the Christian life in our own strength. We need to recognize that Christ is the vine. If we have any life, it has come from Him, and if there is any fruit in our lives, it comes from Him. We are sort of connecting rods, as branches connect into the vine and then bear fruit. Christ said that, "Abide in me, and I in you. As the branch cannot bear fruit of itself, except it abide in the vine; no more can ye, except ye abide in me" (John 15:4).

"If they shall fall away" or "having fallen away," it is impossible to renew them to repentance. They can shed tears all they want to, but they have lost their testimony. For example, a preacher came and talked to me about his situation. He moved away from this area and attempted to establish a ministry. But he failed. He had had an affair with a woman, and he had lost his testimony. He was through. "It is impossible to renew them again unto repentance." I don't question his salvation; he is a gifted man who could be mightily used by God but is not. "Seeing they crucify to themselves the Son of God afresh, and put him to an open shame." My friend, any time you as a born-again child

of God live like one of the Devil's children, you are crucifying the
Son of God—because He came to give you a perfect redemption and to
enable you by the indwelling of the Holy Spirit to be filled with the
Spirit and live for Him.

"For the land which hath drunk the rain that cometh oft upon it,
and bringeth forth herbs meet for them for whose sake it is also tilled,
receiveth blessing from God" (v. 7, ASV). The garden produce is a
blessing to man—my, it is delicious! "But if it beareth thorns and this-
tles, it is rejected and nigh unto a curse; whose end is to be burned"
(v. 8, ASV). "Rejected" is *adokimos,* the same word Paul used when
writing to the Corinthian believers, "But I keep under my body, and
bring it into subjection: lest that by any means, when I have preached
to others, I myself should be a castaway" (1 Cor. 9:27). "Castaway" is
the same word *adokimos,* meaning "not approved." In effect, Paul is
saying, "When I come into His presence I don't want to be disap-
proved. I don't want the Lord Jesus to say to me, 'You have failed. Your
life should have been a testimony but it was not.'" Oh, my friend, you
are going to hear that if you are not living for Him! I know we don't
want to hear these things, but we need to face the facts.

Now notice the key to this chapter: "But, beloved, we are persuaded better things of you, and things that accompany salvation,
though we thus speak" (v. 9). The writer to the Hebrew believers is
saying, "I am persuaded that you are going to live for God, that you are
not going to remain babes in Christ but will grow up."

**For God is not unrighteous to forget your work and la-
bour of love, which ye have shewed toward his name, in
that ye have ministered to the saints, and do minister
[Heb. 6:10].**

"Work and labour of love" won't save you, but if you are saved, this is
why you are rewarded. This is where good works come in. Although
they have nothing to do with your salvation, they certainly do have a
very important part in a believer's life.

And we desire that every one of you do shew the same diligence to the full assurance of hope unto the end [Heb. 6:11].

We need that "full assurance of hope unto the end."

That ye be not slothful, but followers of them who through faith and patience inherit the promises [Heb. 6:12].

God has made a lot of promises to us if we are faithful to Him.

For when God made promise to Abraham, because he could swear by no greater, he sware by himself [Heb. 6:13].

As you know, when you take an oath, you take it on something greater than you are. Since there is nothing greater than God, He swore by Himself.

Saying, Surely blessing I will bless thee, and multiplying I will multiply thee [Heb. 6:14].

God promised that to Abraham (see Gen. 22:15–18; Heb. 11:19).

And so, after he had patiently endured, he obtained the promise [Heb. 6:15].

There is something here that is quite wonderful. Abraham patiently endured, and a new assurance came by trusting God. When you trust God, you walk with Him. You grow in grace and in the knowledge of Him through the study of His Word. This brings you to a place of assurance that cannot be gainsaid.

For men verily swear by the greater: and an oath for confirmation is to them an end of all strife [Heb. 6:16].

When men confirm a statement with an oath, it is an end of every dispute.

> **Wherein God, willing more abundantly to shew unto the heirs of promise the immutability of his counsel, confirmed it by an oath [Heb. 6:17].**

When God does a thing like this, He doesn't need to take an oath, but He does take one to make it very clear how all-important it is.

> **That by two immutable things, in which it was impossible for God to lie, we might have a strong consolation, who have fled for refuge to lay hold upon the hope set before us [Heb. 6:18].**

"That by two immutable things"—what are the two immutable (or unchangeable) things? The Lord promised Abram descendants as innumerable as the stars of heaven (see Gen. 15:4–5), then later He confirmed His promise with an oath (see Gen. 22:16–18). God confirmed His unchangeable Word of promise by a second unchangeable thing, His oath. These two immutable things gave Abraham encouragement and assurance.

Now what are the two immutable things for us today? Not only do we have the promise made to Abraham for our encouragement, but we have a far richer revelation of God's love—the gift of His Son. The (1) death and resurrection of Christ and (2) His ascension and intercession for us are the two immutable things.

These four great facts give us an assurance and provide a refuge that we can lay hold upon.

"Who have fled for refuge to lay hold upon the hope set before us." This reminds us of the cities of refuge which God provided for the children of Israel (see Num. 35; Deut. 19; Josh. 20—21). Those cities of refuge serve as types of Christ sheltering the sinner from death. It was a very marvelous provision for a man who accidentally killed someone. Maybe the one whom he killed had a hot-headed brother who wanted vengeance. So the fugitive could escape to a city of refuge where he would be protected and his case tried. If he was acquitted of intentional killing, he must remain within the city until the death of the high priest.

What a picture this is for us today! This reveals that Christ is our refuge. My friend, I have already been carried into court, and at the trial I was found guilty. I was a sinner. The penalty which was leveled against me was death—and it has already been executed. Christ bore the penalty for me, you see. Because He died in my place, I am free. I have been delivered from the penalty of sin; never do I have to answer for it again. I am free now to go out and serve Him. I now have a High Priest, a resurrected Savior, to whom I can go. What a wonderful picture of my Savior this gives! The apostle Paul wrote to the Corinthians: "Now all these things happened unto them for ensamples: and they are written for our admonition, upon whom the ends of the world are come" (1 Cor. 10:11). "Ensamples" are *types*, and Melchizedek is a type of Christ. Millions of things could have been recorded, but God chose to record only these things because they enable us to grow in our understanding of Him and our relationship to Him.

> **Which hope we have as an anchor of the soul, both sure and stedfast, and which entereth into that within the veil;**
>
> **Whither the forerunner is for us entered, even Jesus, made an high priest for ever after the order of Melchisedec [Heb. 6:19–20].**

When Christ ascended back to heaven, He assumed the office of High Priest.

"Entereth into that within the veil." Christ as High Priest entered into the temple in heaven (after which the earthly tabernacle was patterned, Hebrews 8:5). He passed through the veil into the Holy of Holies, into the presence of God, and presented His blood there. Then He "sat down at the right hand of the Majesty on high."

Now one difference between Aaron and the Lord Jesus is (and I say this reverently) that poor old Aaron never did sit down. There were no seats in the tabernacle—there was the mercy seat, but that typified

God's throne. Aaron only hurried in and hurried out. But you and I have a superior High Priest. He has gone in. He has sat down. He has a *finished* redemption.

Jesus Christ is the "forerunner," which implies that others are to follow.

"As an anchor of the soul." We have an even stronger encouragement than Abraham had in his time because our High Priest has entered in advance into the presence of God for us, and He is there today interceding for us.

CHAPTER 7

THEME: Christ our High Priest after the order of Melchizedek

The rest of the Epistle to the Hebrews deals with the subject of the living Christ who is at this moment at God's right hand. It is a subject that is really neglected in the church today. We talk a great deal about the death and resurrection of Christ—and that is wonderful—but my friend, we need to go on to a *living* Christ who is at God's right hand and who has a ministry there for us. Now the reality of that ministry to us is what is going to test our spiritual life. Here is a barometer or Geiger counter which you can put down on your life: how is the truth of this chapter of Hebrews going to affect your spiritual life?

The writer to the Hebrews is going to make a comparison and contrast of the priesthood of Melchizedek and the priesthood of Aaron.

CHRIST IS PERPETUAL PRIEST

For this Melchisedec, king of Salem, priest of the most high God, who met Abraham returning from the slaughter of the kings, and blessed him [Heb. 7:1].

The little word *for* is used by the writer to the Hebrews as cement to hold together what has been said previously and what he is now going to say. It refers us back to verse 20 of chapter 6. Melchizedek is a type of Christ. In the historical record Melchizedek is called "king of Salem" and "priest of the most high God" (see Genesis 14:17–24). Not much is said about Melchizedek in Genesis 14—frankly, I would have forgotten about him, but the Spirit of God didn't forget about him. When we come to Psalm 110 there is this prophecy concerning the Messiah, the Lord Jesus Christ: ". . . Thou are a priest for ever after the order of Melchizedek" (Ps. 110:4).

You and I are living in the day of Christ's priesthood. There are many critics today who do not like the term *dispensations*. Many preachers won't mention the word. I mention it because the Bible uses the term. Dispensations are the different ages or time-periods showing the progressive order of God's dealing with the human family. This is an example: Back in the Old Testament Aaron was the high priest, and there was a literal tabernacle down here. Today we have a High Priest, but He is not ministering in any building down here. He is up yonder at God's right hand, and He is there right now.

While there are not many references to Melchizedek in the Old Testament, there are quite a few references to him right here in the Epistle to the Hebrews. In Hebrews 5:10 we read, "Called of God an high priest after the order of Melchisedec." Then again in Hebrews 6:20, "Whither the forerunner is for us entered, even Jesus, made an high priest for ever after the order of Melchisedec." Now here in verse 1 the writer says, "For this Melchisedec, king of Salem, priest of the most high God, who met Abraham returning from the slaughter of the kings, and blessed him." He is going to talk a great deal about Melchizedek in this chapter. The very key to this chapter is found in verse 17: "For he testifieth, Thou art a priest for ever after the order of Melchisedec."

Since we are going to look at Christ as a priest after the order of Melchizedek, we need to know all we can about Melchizedek, and we need to go back to the account in Genesis 14. The events of Genesis 14 took place after Sodom, and we have in this chapter the first account of a war. The kings of the east formed a confederacy and came against the kings of the west, that is, those who lived around the Dead Sea. The kings of the east won and lugged off the people as slaves and the wealth of the cities as booty.

Word was brought to Abraham that Lot was being carried away into captivity. Abraham immediately armed about 318 men out of his own household, which means he had quite a household. Each man that he could arm must have had at least one woman and a child. Therefore Abraham must have had about a thousand people who served under him! He took these 318 men, and by a surprise attack he was able to get a victory over the kings of the east. All he was concerned about was rescuing Lot, but in so doing he was able to rescue the king of Sodom and all the others.

In Genesis 14:17 we are told: "And the king of Sodom went out to meet him after his return from the slaughter of Cherdorlaomer, and of the kings that were with him at the valley of Shaveh, which is the king's dale." The king of Sodom made Abraham an offer which he refused, then out of nowhere we read: "And Melchizedek king of Salem brought forth bread and wine: and he was the priest of the most high God" (Gen. 14:18).

> **To whom also Abraham gave a tenth part of all; first being by interpretation King of righteousness, and after that also King of Salem, which is, King of peace [Heb. 7:2].**

It has been supposed by some that Salem was Jerusalem. I do not think that is true at all. Salem is not a place—the word *salem* means "peace." He does not say the Melchizedek was king of Jerusalem. He was king of peace; he was a man who could make peace in that day. I am sure he was king of a literal city somewhere, but it doesn't mean he was king of Jerusalem—it could have been any place. He was king of peace.

Melchizedek was also the "King of righteousness." That is what the name Melchizedek means: *melek* is a Hebrew word meaning "king," and *tsedeq* means "righteousness." Jeremiah speaks of *Jehovah-tsidkenu*, meaning "Jehovah our righteousness."

Melchizedek is a type of Christ—he represents Him in several different ways. He is king of peace and king of righteousness. The Lord Jesus Christ is a King. He is righteousness—He was made unto us righteousness.

Melchizedek was "priest of the most high God." The Lord Jesus is our Great High Priest.

Now the very interesting thing is that when Melchizedek came out to meet Abraham, he brought bread and wine. I believe that these two Old Testament worthies, these patriarchs, celebrated the Lord's Sup-

per together! They were looking forward to the coming of Christ two
thousand years before He came. Today you and I meet and partake of
bread and wine, looking back to the coming of Christ two thousand
years ago. They celebrated the Lord's Supper together. Don't ask me to
explain it—I can't explain it; I can just call your attention to it. This is
something before which we stand in profound awe and wonder and
worship. This is where faith treads on the high places.

> **Without father, without mother, without descent, having
> neither beginning of days, nor end of life; but made like
> unto the Son of God; abideth a priest continually [Heb.
> 7:3].**

Here Melchizedek is a picture of Christ and a type of Christ in another
way. The Lord Jesus comes out of eternity, and He moves into eternity.
He has no beginning and no end. He *is* the beginning. He *is* the end.
You can't go beyond Him in the past, and you can't get ahead of Him
in the future. He encompasses all of time and all of eternity. Now how
can you find a man who pictures that? Melchizedek is in the Book of
Genesis, a book that gives pedigrees—it tells us that Adam begat so-
and-so, and so-and-so begat so-and-so, Abraham begat Isaac, Isaac begat Jacob and Esau, and you follow the genealogies on down—it is a
book of families. Yet in this book that gives the genealogies, Melchizedek just walks out onto the pages of Scripture, out of nowhere, then he
walks off the pages of Scripture, and we do not see him anymore, Why
did God leave out the genealogy of Melchizedek? Because Melchizedek was to be a type of the Lord Jesus in His priesthood. From the
prophecy given in Psalm 110 we see that Melchizedek is a picture of
Christ in that the Lord Jesus is the *eternal* God, and He is a priest
because He is the Son of God, and He is a priest continually. That is,
He just keeps on being a priest—there will be no change in His priesthood because He is eternal.

In the Genesis account we see that Melchizedek came to Abraham
at just the right moment. Abraham was about to be tested, and he
needed someone to encourage him and to strengthen him. Melchizedek came with bread and wine, and he was the priest of "the most

high God." (This is the first time in Scripture that God is called "the most high God.") He came just as the king of Sodom was making a proposition to Abraham: "Now Abraham, it was nice of you to recover Lot and the rest of the people, and we appreciate that. I know you don't want to make the people slaves; so give us the people, and you keep the booty. You keep it, Abraham, it's yours." Now according to the Code of Hammurabi for that day, the booty did belong to Abraham, but Abraham said, "Why, I wouldn't do that at all. I won't take even a shoestring from you—not even a thread. I refuse to receive anything from you" (see Gen. 14:23].Then God appeared to Abraham and said, "I am thy shield, and thy exceeding great reward" (Gen. 15:1).

Melchizedek came and ministered to Abraham. The Lord Jesus Christ is the Great High Priest, and He ministers to us today. I will be very frank with you, if He doesn't minister to you and bless your heart and life, it is because you are still a litle babe and you haven't grown up. You have not entered into the great truth presented here. My Christian friend, have you gone through trials and deep waters, and has Jesus ministered to you and helped you? Are you conscious of the fact that He blesses you every day?

On one tour that I conducted to Bible lands, I left half-sick and would not have gone if my wife had not urged me to do so. I just didn't feel up to the trip. On the trip I was sick several times and had to drop out of the tour a couple of days. But God was so good to us. We had good weather; we never had a bad flight, and the Lord was just good to me in so many ways. I was conscious of the fact that my High Priest was on the job; He was doing His job, my friend, and He was blessing. I'm talking to you about reality. I'm not talking to you about a theory, about a religion, or about a ritual that you go through. I'm talking to you about a Man in the glory who is alive, and He is the living God. Is He the living God to you?

Notice what it says in Genesis 14:19—"And he [Melchizedek] blessed him, and said, Blessed be Abram of the most high God, possessor of heaven and earth." You and I live in a universe that belongs to Him; He owns it, and He has said that all things are ours today. Do you enjoy a sunrise? Just this morning I went by myself out to a nearby golf course, and I saw the sun come up over the Sierra Madre mountains.

He did that just for me this morning. What a performance He put on. He is wonderful! What a glorious day it is! He is the living Christ. I just thanked Him again for bringing me to another day, and I thanked Him for being so good to me, and I told Him that I love Him. The living Christ is yonder at God's right hand. How real is He to you?

CHRIST IS PERFECT PRIEST

Now consider how great this man was, unto whom even the patriarch Abraham gave the tenth of the spoils [Heb. 7:4].

Abraham paid tithes to Melchizedek. He recognized that Melchizedek was above him and that he was the priest of the most high God.

And verily they that are of the sons of Levi, who receive the office of the priesthood, have a commandment to take tithes of the people according to the law, that is, of their brethren, though they come out of the loins of Abraham [Heb. 7:5].

In Abraham the sons of Levi, who were descended from Abraham, paid tithes to Melchizedek. This shows that Melchizedek was superior to Aaron and his family.

My friend, one of the ways in which you recognize the lordship of Jesus Christ is by coming and making a gift to Him. Every gift ought to be more than just to a church or to some other ministry; it should be a gift to the Lord Jesus Christ. You recognize His lordship, and you are a priest worshipping when you bring a gift to Him.

But he whose descent is not counted from them received tithes of Abraham, and blessed him that had the promises [Heb. 7:6].

You would think that Abraham would be superior to Melchizedek, but he was not. Melchizedek was a Gentile who was the priest of the most high God. I do not know where he got his information about God, nor do I know the background of this man. If anyone tries to tell you more about him, he is guessing. Also there are a whole lot of things I can't explain about the Lord Jesus because He is *God*. I do know that He is my Great High Priest today—and that's all I need to know.

And without all contradiction the less is blessed of the better [Heb. 7:7].

Abraham was blessed by Melchizedek who was better than he was. When you and I worship the Lord Jesus and bow before Him, we recognize His superiority.

And here men that die receive tithes; but there he receiveth them, of whom it is witnessed that he liveth [Heb. 7:8].

"Here men that die" refers to the Levitical priests; "but there he" refers to Melchizedek.

You can offer yourself to Him, and He will receive you. When I offer myself to Him, He doesn't get much, but I have offered myself to Him and am thankful that he will accept me.

And as I may so say, Levi also, who receiveth tithes, payed tithes in Abraham.

For he was yet in the loins of his father, when Melchisedec met him [Heb. 7:9–10].

"Levi also, who receiveth tithes, payed tithes in Abraham." The priestly tribe of Levi was in the loins of Abraham when he paid tithes to Melchizedek, and thus Levi also paid tithes to Melchizedek. In the same way, back yonder when Adam sinned, I also sinned. In Adam all died. The reason you and I are going to die, if the Lord tarries His coming, is that we are in Adam and we sinned in Adam. However, today I am perfect because I am in Christ. Do you realize that? God sees me in Christ, and I am perfect in Him. I am accepted in the Beloved. My friend, this is great scriptural truth, and it is stated in simple language.

> **If therefore perfection were by the Levitical priesthood, (for under it the people received the law,) what further need was there that another priest should rise after the order of Melchisedec, and not be called after the order of Aaron? [Heb. 7:11].**

In other words, the thing which characterized the Aaronic priesthood is that it was incomplete. It never brought perfection, complete communion with God. It never gave redemption and acceptance before God to the people. It never achieved its goal. Therefore we need Christ.

> **For the priesthood being changed, there is made of necessity a change also of the law [Heb. 7:12].**

We are not under the Mosaic Law. The Mosaic Law belonged to the Aaronic priesthood where they offered bloody sacrifices. The Mosaic Law and the Aaronic priesthood go together.

> **For he of whom these things are spoken pertaineth to another tribe, of which no man gave attendance at the altar.**
>
> **For it is evident that our Lord sprang out of Juda; of which tribe Moses spake nothing concerning priesthood [Heb. 7:13–14].**

The Lord Jesus came in the tribe of Judah and therefore could never be a priest here on earth. The priestly tribe was the tribe of Levi. The priesthood had to be changed since Christ did not come from Levi.

> **And it is yet far more evident: for that after the similitude of Melchisedec there ariseth another priest [Heb. 7:15].**

This is what the prophecy in Psalm 110 said concerning the Messiah who was to come.

> **Who is made, not after the law of a carnal command-ment, but after the power of an endless life.**

> **For he testifieth, Thou art a priest for ever after the order of Melchisedec [Heb. 7:16–17].**

Christ became a priest by His resurrection from the dead; He has an endless life.

> **For there is verily a disannulling of the commandment going before for the weakness and unprofitableness thereof [Heb. 7:18].**

The Mosaic system went out of style—it wore out. It never gave what man must have: perfection.

> **For the law made nothing perfect, but the bringing in of a better hope did; by the which we draw nigh unto God [Heb. 7:19].**

We come to God through Christ. We have seen that the Lord Jesus Christ is a perpetual priest and He is a perfect priest. The Aaronic priesthood could not fill the bill. Now we have a perfect priest, and that one is the Lord Jesus Christ. He has provided salvation for you and me. God has taken us out of Adam and put us in Christ. "Therefore if any man be in Christ, he is a new creature: old things are passed away; behold, all things are become new" (2 Cor. 5:17). We are no longer joined to Adam but are now joined to the living Christ.

We will summarize the contrast between the priesthood of Aaron and the priesthood of Melchizedek as follows:

Law vs. Power
(law restrains—power enables)

Commandment *(external)* vs. Life *(internal)*
Carnal *(flesh)* vs. Endless *(eternal life)*
Changing vs. Unchanging
Weakness and unprofitableness vs. Nigh to God
Nothing perfect vs. Better hope

And inasmuch as not without an oath he was made priest:

(For those priests were made without an oath; but this with an oath by him that said unto him, The Lord sware and will not repent, Thou art a priest for ever after the order of Melchisedec:) [Heb. 7:20–21].

In Psalm 110 is a prophecy of the fact that the Messiah, the Lord Jesus Christ, would be in the line of Melchizedek as priest. "The LORD hath sworn, and will not repent, Thou art a priest for ever after the order of Melchizedek" (Ps. 110:4). One thing that makes the priesthood of Christ superior is the very simple fact that it rests not only upon the Word of God but upon the *oath* of God. All the Old Testament tells us of the tribe of Levi is that they were set aside for that particular function—no oath was given concerning them.

By so much was Jesus made a surety of a better testament [Heb. 7:22].

The word *testament* should be "covenant." We have not only a better priesthood in Jesus Christ, but it is also by a better covenant. Christ is our High Priest. He ministers in a superior sanctuary, by a better covenant, and built upon better promises—we will see this subject expanded in chapters 8 through 10. The Lord Jesus' priesthood is superior in every department.

CHRIST IN HIS PERSON IS PERPETUAL AND PERFECT PRIEST

And they truly were many priests, because they were not suffered to continue by reason of death [Heb. 7:23].

In other words, the Aaronic priesthood of the Old Testament always ended by death. Aaron died, just as Moses did. I have always felt that the death of Aaron—if it wasn't greater—was just as great a loss to Israel as the death of Moses. In his death they lost their high priest, the one who had gone with them through the wilderness, the one who knew them and understood them. Now they would have to have a new priest. You and I don't have a changing priesthood—Christ will always live to make intercession for us.

> **But this man, because he continueth ever, hath an unchangeable priesthood [Heb. 7:24].**

The Lord Jesus won't be dying anymore. He died once for our sins, but never again will He die. He is there all the time for you.

I received a letter once from a man in Puerto Rico who comes home late at night from his work in an oil refinery. He listens every night at 11:30 to our radio Bible study program. The Spirit of God ministers the Word of God to him down there late at night. The Lord Jesus knew all about that man long before I got his letter and learned of him. I didn't know him, and I didn't know he was listening to the radio broadcast. The Lord Jesus knew all about him because He has an unchangeable priesthood. He is on duty twenty-four hours a day. That means that at 11:30 at night He knows this man, understands him, and ministers the Word of God to him. I rejoice in being able to give out the Word of God today because I am assured that the Spirit of God will be ministering it to folk. The Lord Jesus is the Great High Priest. While that fellow was listening, I was asleep in bed on the other side of the continent. But while I am sleeping there is a High Priest up yonder who will make the Word effective. How wonderful this is! Let's give Him all the praise and glory.

The following verse is perhaps the key verse to this entire section, and it is the very heart of the Gospel.

> **Wherefore he is able also to save them to the uttermost that come unto God by him, seeing he ever liveth to make intercession for them [Heb. 7:25].**

"Wherefore"—again we have this little hinge on which a big door swings. It swings back into what has been said before and swings on into what is ahead.

"He ever liveth." It says, first of all, that Christ is not dead, but He is living. Right at this very moment He is alive. We emphasize the death and resurrection of Christ, but we ought to go beyond that. We have to do with a *living* Christ. We know Him no longer after the flesh. We know Him today as our Great High Priest at God's right hand. My friend, that is where we need to put the emphasis. He died down here to save us, but He *lives* up there to keep us saved.

"He is able also to save them to the uttermost that come unto God by him." He is able to keep on saving you. "To the uttermost" means all the way through. He is able to save us completely and perfectly. He is the Great Shepherd who up to this very moment has never lost a sheep. Do you want to know something? He *never will* lose one. If you are one of His sheep, you may feel like you are going to be lost, but He is up there for you and He is watching over you.

"He ever liveth to make intercession." *Intercession* actually means "intervention." He intervenes for us. ". . . We shall be saved by his life" (Rom. 5:10). John wrote, "My little children [born ones], these things write I unto you, that ye sin not." Well, John, you are not talking to *me* because I do lots of things that are wrong. Now, John, do you have a word for me? John went on to say, "And if any man sin"—now we are getting somewhere!—"we have an advocate with the Father, Jesus Christ the righteous" (1 John 2:1). An advocate is a *paraclete*, a comforter, someone to stand at our side. He is Jesus Christ the righteous. Everything He does is right. Everything He does is righteous. We shall be saved by His life.

How wonderful to know we have a living Christ! You are not alone, my friend. It is just baby stuff to sit down and cry, "Oh, I'm having this problem, and I'm so alone. There's nobody to help me. To whom shall I go?" My friend, what do you think He is doing up there? Aren't you conscious of Him? Why don't you turn to Him?

I remember talking to the mother of a man who was leaving his wife and running away with another woman. I took the mother with me when I went to talk with the other woman. She would not change her mind and was determined to go with this man. This poor mother, as I took her home, just got down on the floor of the car and began to cry out, "Oh, God, why have you forsaken me?" But by the time I got her home, she was more composed and apologized, "I'm sorry I said that God has forsaken me. I don't believe that He has." I assured her that we can be sure of the fact that He ever lives to make intercession for us. Though we are faithless, He is always faithful to us. It is wonderful to know He is up there, my friend.

> **For such an high priest became us, who is holy, harmless, undefiled, separate from sinners, and made higher than the heavens [Heb. 7:26].**

He "became us" means Christ is just what we need. He is the one who fills the bill. He is just right for us—we couldn't have anyone better than He is.

"Holy"—that is, in relationship to God. He is the holy one.

"Harmless" means that He is free from any malice, craftiness, or cleverness. When He gets you off when you sin, it is not because He is a clever lawyer. It is because He is the one who paid the penalty for you, and the penalty absolutely has been paid.

"Undefiled"—He is free from any moral impurity. My friend, this is God's answer to the blasphemous films, songs, and literature of our day. The Bible makes it clear that the Lord Jesus was free from moral impurity.

He is also "separate from sinners." He is like us, yet unlike us. He could mix and mingle with sinners, and they didn't feel uncomfortable in His presence, but He was not one of them. His enemies accused Him of associating with publicans and sinners. He sure did, yet He wasn't one of them. He was separate from sinners.

> **Who needeth not daily, as those high priests, to offer up sacrifice, first for his own sins, and then for the people's: for this he did once, when he offered up himself [Heb. 7:27].**

Notice that the Lord Jesus did not need to offer any sacrifice for His own sin—He had none.

If it were necessary for the Lord Jesus to come back and die for you again, He'd be back, my friend. He would be back today. But He won't be back to die for you—He died once.

The continual sacrificing in the Old Testament must have gotten pretty old and pretty tiresome. I am sure that many times when the priests would meet there at the laver to wash their hands and feet, one of them would turn to the other and say, "How many times have you been here today?"

"Well, I don't know. I'm sure I have been here at least a dozen times."

The other would reply, "Well, I have been here fifteen times. I've washed my hands here so many times that I've got dishpan hands! And look at my feet—they look like I've been standing in water all day. I'm so tired of going to that altar and offering sacrifices again and again and again."

I want to tell you, it must have been pretty wearisome, and if Aaron had overheard them talking, I think he would have said, "I agree with you that this ritual gets tiresome, but do you know what God is trying to tell us? He is trying to tell us that sin is an awful thing and that it requires the shedding of blood. But He has One who is coming some-day who is going to die on a cross for us. When He does, there is going to be no more shedding of blood. He will have paid the penalty."

For the law maketh men high priests which have infirmity; but the word of the oath, which was since the law, maketh the Son, who is consecrated for evermore [Heb. 7:28].

The high priest in the Old Testament had to offer a sacrifice for himself—the Lord Jesus never did.

We have a High Priest who can be touched, who can be reached today. He is there to help and He understands, but He is holy, harmless, undefiled, and separate from sinners.

APPENDIX

THEME: The authorship of Hebrews or did Paul write Hebrews?; internal evidences on authorship; date and destination; arguments available on authorship; a defense of the Pauline authorship

THE AUTHORSHIP OF HEBREWS OR DID PAUL WRITE HEBREWS?

The Epistle to the Hebrews presents many moot problems. Some of them are in conjunction with the question of authorship, which we shall consider under the following divisions:
1. Internal evidence on authorship
   (Is Hebrews an epistle or treatise?)
2. Date and Destination
3. Arguments available on authorship
4. A defense of the Pauline authorship

It is evident that we are contending for the Pauline authorship of Hebrews. First we shall present all arguments against it, as indicated by the headings. Then we shall present the evidence that establishes the Pauline authorship in our own thinking.

INTERNAL EVIDENCES ON AUTHORSHIP

The deciding factor in determining the authorship, according to one writer, is that tradition and history shed no light upon the question of the authorship of Hebrews. This probably is being considered first because we do not agree with the writer on this statement. Rather, we believe that both history and tradition lend a deciding voice to this question.

We are therefore thrown back, in our search for the author, on such evidence as the epistle itself affords, and that is wholly inferential. It seems probable that the author was a Hellenist, a

Greek-speaking Jew. He was familiar with the Scriptures of the
OT and with the religious ideas and worship of the Jews. He
claims the inheritance of their sacred history, traditions and in-
stitutions (1:1), and dwells on them with an intimate knowledge and enthusiasm that would be improbable, though not
impossible, in a proselyte, and still more in a Christian convert
from heathenism. But he knew the OT only in the LXX [Septua-
gint] translation, which he follows even where it deviates from
the Hebrew. He writes Greek with a purity of style and vocabu-
lary to which the writings of Luke alone in the NT can be compared. His mind is imbued with that combination of Hebrew
and Greek thought which is best known in the writings of
Philo. His general typological mode of thinking, his use of the
allegorical method, as well as the adoption of many terms that
are most familiar in Alexandrian thought, all reveal the Hellen-
istic mind. Yet his fundamental conceptions are in full accord
with the teaching of Paul and of the Johannine writings.

The central position assigned to Christ, the high estimate of
His person, the saving significance of His death, the general
trend of the ethical teaching, the writer's opposition to asceti-
cism and his esteem for the rulers and teachers of the church,
all bear out the inference that he belonged to a Christian circle
dominated by Pauline ideas. The author and his readers alike
were not personal disciples of Jesus, but had received the gospel from those who had heard the Lord (2:3) and who were no
longer living (13:7). . . . The letter [Paul] quotes the OT from the
Hebrew and LXX but Hebrews only from LXX. . . . For Paul the
OT is law, and stands in antithesis to the NT, but in Hebrews the
OT is covenant, and is the "shadow" of the New Covenant. (*The
International Standard Bible Encyclopedia*, vol. II, p. 1357.)

We have quoted voluminously from this writer because his main thesis
is to show that Paul could not have been the author. His sole proof is
based on the internal evidence from the epistle.

In considering the internal nature of the epistle, a word must be
said relative to the question: Is it really an epistle? There is no word of

salutation or greeting in this Epistle to the Hebrews, such as marks the other New Testament books, with the possible exception of 1 John. It is in the form of a treatise rather than a letter. In it are long, philosophical sentences written in purest idiomatic Greek. It bears no mark of a translation from the Hebrew, as Clement of Alexandria suggests. This is an inference on his part because it was written to Hebrew-speaking Jews. The length of the epistle is another thing that might suggest a treatise, yet note the author's own words in this respect, ". . . for I have written a letter unto you in few words" (Heb. 13:22). Delitzsch has this enlightening comment to make on this epistle:

> We seem at first to have a treatise before us, but the special hortatory reference interwoven with the most discursive and dogmatic portions of the work soon show us that it is really a kind of sermon addressed to some particular and well known auditory; while at the close the homiletic form changes into that of an epistle.

According to Deissmann's definition of an epistle as distinct from a letter, we feel sure that this would allow it to fall under the category of an epistle. Its conclusion is that of an epistle. Later in our discussion we shall present a reason for the omission of a greeting. These problems are intimately tied up with the question of authorship, especially when one attempts to maintain the Pauline authorship. We agree with Plumer that this is an epistle.

As we conclude this section on the internal nature of the Epistle to the Hebrews, we should note that this epistle is in composition and lofty concept the masterpiece of the New Testament, although there is no conclusive evidence for the authorship. Only suggestions and intimations shed light on this problem. In our defense for the Pauline authorship we shall undertake to show that the suggestions and intimations point to Paul as the author, yet we are not dogmatic in stating that the proof is positive.

DATE AND DESTINATION

The latest date for the composition of Hebrews is A.D. 96. The earliest date cannot be determined so easily. It must have been written after

A.D. 50 if it is made dependent on Paul's epistles. All critics fix the
dating between these two terminal points. Moffatt shows that Clement,
Justin Martyr, Hermas, and Tertullian knew of it and quoted from it.
Clement quoted from it at length. By the second century it was widely
circulated and read. Rees places the date around A.D. 80, Moffatt
around A.D. 85. Here is a list of the probable datings: Basnage—A.D.
61; L'Enfant and Beausobre—A.D. 62; Horne and Bagster—A.D. 62 or
63; Pearson, Lardner, Tomlin, Mill, Wetstein, and Tillemont—A.D. 63;
Authorized Version and Lloyd—A.D. 64; Michaelis—A.D. 64–65;
Scott—A.D. 65; Ebrard before A.D. 58. The number of dates given suggests that the means used to arrive at a date was by way of the lottery,
not by process of scholarship. However, Hebrews must have been written before the destruction of Jerusalem in A.D. 70. Because there is
constant reference to the Old Testament ritual being in progress at that
time, certainly there would have been reference to the destruction of
the temple. Having examined the arguments carefully, we are fully
persuaded that those who place the dating of it after the destruction of
Jerusalem do not sufficiently answer the question of why the writer
omitted reference to this catastrophe.

E. Schuyler English gives us this word:

> It is also obvious that the epistle was written before the de-
> struction of Jerusalem in A.D. 70. For at the time of its composi-
> tion Mosaic institutions were still being observed—priests were
> offering gifts according to the Law (8:3–5) and the temple was
> still standing (13:11–12). The temple was in Jerusalem.

Godet has a fitting comment:

> This epistle, without introduction or subscription, is like
> the great High Priest of whom it treats, who was without begin-
> ning of days or end of years, abiding an High Priest continually.
> It is entirely fitting that it should remain anonymous.

The epistle was first accepted by the Eastern church. Athanasius
accepted it, and the council of Carthage confirmed it in A.D. 397.
Paul's name was on the epistle about the time it began to circulate.

The consensus is that Hebrews was written to Jewish Christians. But where were the Jewish Christians located? It was not written for the whole body of Jewish believers everywhere. It was written to a particular church located in a particular place. The epistle bears testimony to this: The church had for some time obeyed the Gospel (Heb. 5:12); past conduct inspired confidence in their sincerity (Heb. 6:9); they had been kind to God's people (Heb. 6:10); note other personal references in Hebrews 10:32–34; 13:19, 23. Was this church in Palestine or out of Palestine? It is around this question that the argument on destination is based.

First of all, there is evidence that the first readers were Jews. The epistle assumes an intimate knowledge with the Old Testament. The readers were of the same lineage as Jews in the Old Testament (Heb. 1:1; 3:9). Zahn has this comment to make:

> Hebrews does not contain a single sentence in which it is so much as intimated that the readers became members of God's people who descended from Abraham, and heirs of the promise given to them and their forefathers, and how they became such. 13:13 shows that both the readers and author were members of the Jewish race.

Now we shall try to determine whom or rather what particular church the author was addressing. This epistle is addressed to the *Hebrews*, which word in the New Testament does not apply to all Jews. It was used for those who were more thoroughly of Jewish origins and habits and who spoke the vernacular of Palestine. The other Jews outside of Palestine were designated Hellenists. Lindsay says that Acts 6:1 makes this distinction clear. DeWette says that Eusebius, speaking of the Jews of Asia Minor, styles them not Hebrews but *ex Hebraion ontes*. Chrysostom says that this epistle was sent to Jerusalem. The fact that the epistle was written in Greek does not negate the evidence that it was sent to Palestine, for it is natural for a writer out of Palestine to write in the universal language of his day. The Palestinian Jews were well acquainted with Greek, as Deissmann has clearly demonstrated. In fact, it was the language of communication. DeWette held to the opinion that this epistle was destined to parts other than Palestine; yet he acknowledges that the Jewish character of the epistle—the persecutions which they were enduring, the consequent risk of apostasy, and the ancient opinion—reveal Palestine as the more probable destination. Ebrard wrote, "We are at liberty to seek these Jewish Christians only in Jerusalem."

ARGUMENTS AVAILABLE ON AUTHORSHIP

We can say with Shakespeare that we have now come to the very heart of the matter. There is less evidence for the authorship of this epistle than of any other book of the New Testament. Others have problems of authorship, but there is some definite evidence available and some general agreement, at least, regarding the author. For example, nearly all critics say that some John wrote the fourth Gospel. But there is no such agreement regarding Hebrews. Moffatt rightly says that few characters in the New Testament have escaped the attention of those in late days who have sought to identify them as the author of Hebrews. Apollos, Peter, Philip, Silvanus, Prisca, Barnabas, and Paul have all been suggested as the possible author. To Moffatt's list we might add the names of Luke, Silas, Clement of Rome, Ariston, and Titus, all of whom have been suggested as the possible author. Out of this dozen, one is privileged to take his choice—or refrain from doing so, as Moffatt does. Moffatt concludes that the author was one of those unknown personalities in whom the early church was more rich than we realize. There is absolutely no basis, other than conjecture, for asserting that most of these were the author, although several have a plausible claim.

As we examine their claim to authorship, Luke and Clement are easily eliminated because a comparison of their writings to the Epistle to the Hebrews reveals a difference in style, composition, and influence. Clement quotes from Hebrews, and his own writings show marked differences. (See introduction of Moffatt's commentary on Hebrews.) So little is known of the others, with the exception of Barnabas, that it is impossible to establish a case for or against them. Barnabas will be considered in the three theories that are presented.

In the early church were three traditions regarding the authorship of Hebrews: The Alexandrian tradition supported the Pauline author-ship; the African tradition supported the authorship of Barnabas; Rome and the West supported the idea that it was anonymous.

1. *Alexandrian tradition:* Clement says that his teacher, probably Pantaenus, explained why Paul did not address his readers under his name. He further states that Paul wrote it in Hebrew and Luke trans-lated it into Greek. Origen follows Clement, but knowing that the view of Alexandria was criticized, he concludes that the author is "known only to God." By the fourth century the tradition of the Pauline author-ship was well established in Alexandria, Syria, and Greece. This tra-dition prevailed until the revival of learning. Eusebius favored the Pauline tradition, as did Dionysius of Alexandria, Alexander of Alex-andria, Athanasius, Cyril of Jerusalem, Epiphanius, the Council of Laodicea of A.D. 363, and Erasmus. Among those who denied the Paul-ine tradition were Irenaeus, Cyprian of Carthage, Tertullian, Caius and Novatus, presbyters of the church at Rome. Calvin did not accept the tradition, for he says, "I, indeed, can deduce no reason to show that Paul was its author." Luther and Moll defend the authorship of Apollos against the Pauline tradition. Thus we see that tradition was probably equally divided.

2. *African tradition:* This view supported Barnabas as the author of Hebrews. Tertullian was the leading exponent, for he attributed the epistle, without question, to Barnabas. This is the most tempting sug-gestion, as Wickham remarks. It suits the character of Barnabas. Barnabas was a "Levite of the country of Cyprus," a Hellenist by birth-place, but a Hebrew by race, interested in the sacrificial system, com-panion of Paul (yet one who entertained views of his own), the "son of consolation," the mediator and peacemaker between old and new. Zahn infers that this tradition arose in Montanist churches and origi-nates in Asia. However, this tradition was superseded by the Alexan-drian tradition, for in A.D. 393 the council of Hippo reckoned thirteen epistles to Paul, but in A.D. 419 the council of Carthage reckoned four-teen to Paul, which would include Hebrews.

3. *Roman tradition:* This view said the author was anonymous. No tradition of authorship appears before A.D. 400, according to Rees. Stephen Gobarus, writing in A.D. 600, says that both Irenaeus and Hip-

polytus denied the Pauline authorship. The epistle was known to Clement of Rome, and he mentions no one as author. Another suggestion as to the authorship of Hebrews is mentioned by Plumer. It is that of Zemas, the lawyer. This makes thirteen guesses as to the author of Hebrews.

A DEFENSE OF THE PAULINE AUTHORSHIP

We are not holding dogmatically or tenaciously to an obsolete view. Rather, we have examined the evidence and find no reason to reject the Pauline authorship. It is not our purpose in this section to affirm that Paul wrote Hebrews, but to set forth our reasons for tentatively accepting the Pauline authorship, or the authority, that this epistle rests upon, for the canonicity of this epistle depends largely upon the view of authorship. It was accepted into the canon on Pauline authority; and with that removed, it is possible to reject this great epistle.

Under the first heading (Internal Evidences on Authorship) we attempted to show that all the light from the epistle itself reveals only the fact that the author is anonymous. His name is nowhere mentioned in the epistle. Now, using the internal evidence, we want to show how Paul *could be* the author.

So far we have tried to show two things: (1) there is no evidence, external or internal, to support any claim as to the authorship, except it be Paul; (2) there is nothing incompatible with thinking that Paul wrote it.

Now we shall take our third burden of proof and attempt to show that internal and external evidence support the Pauline authorship.

1. *Internal Evidence:* Origen remarked that the thoughts (*noemata*) of this epistle all bore the stamp of Paul's mind, but the language was *Hellenikotera*, purer Greek than his. Following is Lindsay's list of representations and images which are found in Hebrews and in Paul's other epistles, which are not found in the works of other New Testament writers.

Compare Heb. 1:1, 3 with 2 Cor. 4:4; Col. 1:15–16.

Compare Heb. 1:4; 2:9 with Phil. 2:8–9.

Compare Heb. 2:14 with 1 Cor. 15:54, 57.

Compare Heb. 7:16, 18–19 with Rom. 2:29; Gal. 3:3, 24.
Compare Heb. 7:26 with Eph. 4:10.
Compare Heb. 8:5; 10:1 with Col. 2:17.
Compare Heb. 10:12–13 with 1 Cor. 15:25.

DeWette and Bleek have concluded that since Hebrews reads more like Paul's writing than any other New Testament writings, it was written by a disciple of Paul. The opponents of the Pauline authorship are quoted to show that this book is not unlike Paul's writings and could have been written by Paul. Paul obviously meets this requirement.

Some have claimed that Hebrews 2:3 excludes Paul as the author because he says in Galatians 1:11–12 that he received his Gospel not from men but from God. However, this is not incongruous with Paul's statement in Galatians. Paul is evidently using the editorial "we" that is used so effectually in the New Testament. If Paul places himself in the same category with the other Christians at Jerusalem, he could not say that we received it from God on the road to Damascus about midday on a mule. Paul's conversion was peculiar to himself. Then the Galatians passage does not exclude the fact that Paul did not have it confirmed unto him by the ones who heard the Lord. In Galatians he is defending his apostleship and is therefore showing from whence he received his authority.

As to the statement that Hebrews 13:7 reveals that the apostles were no longer living at the time Hebrews was written, we can hardly see where this verse establishes any such view.

Regarding the fact that the Epistle to the Hebrews quotes the Old Testament from the Septuagint Version, it is possible for Paul to have quoted only from the Septuagint in Hebrews and from both the Septuagint and the Hebrew in his other epistles. The fact that there are more quotations in this book than in any other New Testament book shows that the author is placing a great deal of stress on these quotations. Instead of quoting from memory, he would have a copy of the Old Testament at hand. Paul did quote from the Septuagint frequently, and he could easily have used it exclusively in the Epistle to the Hebrews.

Rees says that Paul's Christology turns about the death, resurrection, and living presence of Christ in the church. In contrast, the Epistle to the Hebrews centers about the high priestly nature of Christ's

work. He evidently is thinking of Ephesians, Colossians,
1 Corinthians, and Romans, for the rest of Paul's epistles deal no more
with these subjects than does Hebrews. This method of trying to dis-
tinguish different authors by difference of style is not conclusive, to
say the least. Certainly it is not a valid argument in this epistle.

We come now to the problem of the absence of the author's name in
the Epistle to the Hebrews. Why did the author conceal his name? The
theory has been advanced that had Paul been the author he would have
subscribed his name, and the fact that his name does not appear shows
he did not write it. We submit Plumer's answer to this sort of reasoning:

> Moreover, if Paul is proven not to be its author because it lacks
> his name, the same reasoning would prove it had no author at
> all, for it bears no name whatsoever.

Now let us examine the reasons why Paul might have concealed his
name. Dr. Biesenthal, writing on Hebrews, advances a new and interesting theory for the reason the writer concealed his name. He shows
that Christianity's teaching that animal sacrifices were no longer
needed was being felt in heathendom. Consequently, sacrifices at
births, marriages, and other occasions, were being neglected. The
priestly class, which lived by these sacrifices, and the large cattle in-
dustry, were being threatened by utter ruin. This created a great antag-
onism against Christianity. Dr. Biesenthal, a Hebrew by race,
concludes that for this reason the writer withheld his name from this
epistle which so bitterly denounces animal sacrifices.

Also Paul himself was a man who was hated by the Jewish nation.
To them he was no less than a traitor. This brilliant young Pharisee,
who was well versed in the ritual of Moses, as he himself claims, was
anathema to his brethren in the flesh. In writing to them this learned
work, composed in the best Greek, he withheld the name that would
prevent its circulation among those to whom it was originally destined.

There is another reason we think to be more valid, which was presented even by the Alexandrian tradition. It is that Paul left off his salu-

tation, "Paul, an apostle of Jesus Christ," because he was not the apostle to the Jews but to the Gentiles. Another more recent suggestion on this line comes from a consideration of Hebrews 3:1: ". . . Consider the Apostle and High Priest of our profession, Christ Jesus." Christ is the great Apostle in this epistle and the writer would not subscribe his name beside the one of Christ. Certainly the fact that the writer did not mention his name does not eliminate Paul from the list of possible authors.

There are a few suggestions in the epistle that point to Paul as author. The writer was a Jew acquainted with the details of Mosaic ritualism (Heb. 13:13). He was acquainted with Greek philosophy, or rather, Alexandrian thought. The author of this epistle had been in prison in the locality where the ones addressed resided (Heb. 10:34). He was at that time in prison in Italy (Heb. 13:19, 24). Timothy was his companion and messenger (Heb. 13:23). When Paul was in Rome in prison he used Timothy to carry messages, and he sent him on a trip from the west to the east (Phil. 2:19). The writer hoped to be liberated (Heb. 13:19). This is the same thought that is expressed in Philippians 1:25 and Philemon 22. While these suggestions are not conclusive, who better fits this description than Paul? An appropriate supposition from Lightfoot concludes this section on internal evidence: "The very style of it may argue the scholar of Gamaliel."

The dating of the Epistle to the Hebrews does not conflict with the Pauline authorship. If it were written before the destruction of Jerusalem, which we believe to be correct, it coincides nicely with Paul's imprisonment at Rome. Paul's last visit to Jerusalem helps explain the epistle. The Book of Acts tells us that Paul went up to Jerusalem in spite of the warning of the Spirit. His arrest was the result of having gone into the temple to purify himself with the four men who had a vow. This he was asked to do and to make apparent that he walked orderly and kept the Law. Did he do wrong? This is not a question for us to answer. The point is that he—knowing that he was dead to the Law—acted through zeal and love for his brethren. The believers at Jerusalem still clung to the Law and to the temple. When Paul was in Rome, he wrote this epistle to show these Jews the better things of the New Covenant and to warn them not to be drawn back into Judaism.

This throws a great deal of light on Hebrews 13:13: "Let us go forth therefore unto him without the camp [Judaism], bearing his reproach."

The Spirit of God could have used this epistle for the comfort of Jewish Christians right before the destruction of the temple. We suggest this to show that the dating and destination are not incompatible with the Pauline authorship.

2. *External Evidence:* Several of the early church fathers who favored the Pauline authorship have been mentioned, but we have reserved for this section other evidence that confirms us in our view that Paul wrote Hebrews. This is Origen's statement in full regarding the author of Hebrews.

> The thoughts are Paul's but the phraseology and composition are by someone else. *Not without reason have the ancient men handed down the Epistle as Paul's,* but who wrote the Epistle is known only to God.

We especially note that clause which is italicized. Evidently there was already in Origen's day a tradition that Paul wrote this epistle. Quite evidently it was the opinion of the earliest church in the East that Hebrews was Paul's epistle. It was not until a later day, and by a church more remote from Palestine, that the tradition arose of another author. Jerome, the greatest of the Latin fathers, considered Paul the author. It was during the third and fourth centuries that the Pauline authorship was denied in Rome. It is also interesting to note that during this same period the epistle was held in disrepute. After it regained its place as canonical Scripture, it was also considered as Pauline. Lindsay makes this valuable comment on the Western tradition. Jerome suggests that at first it was received in Rome as Scripture and received also as Pauline. It is significant that both go together.

Others could be mentioned, but they would add nothing decisive either way.

We now turn to a bit of evidence that is enlightening. Peter wrote to those of the circumcision, to believing Jews everywhere. In 2 Peter 3:15 he mentions the fact that Paul had written to them. He separated this epistle from the others of Paul (v. 16). No epistle of Paul other than

Hebrews answers to this statement. If Hebrews is not the epistle, then the epistle to which he refers has been lost.

To conclude our remarks, we quote a statement from Weymouth that illustrates how easy it is to defend a theory and support it with misinformation:

> The only fact clear as to the author is that he was not the Apostle Paul. The early Fathers did not attribute the book to Paul, nor was it until the seventh century that the tendency to do this, derived from Jerome, swelled into an ecclesiastical practice. From the book itself we see that the author must have been a Jew and a Hellenist, familiar with Philo as well as with the Old Testament, a friend of Timothy and well known to many of those whom he addressed, and not an Apostle but decidedly acquainted with Apostolic thoughts; and that he not only wrote before the destruction of Jerusalem but apparently himself was never in Palestine. The name of Barnabas, and also that of Priscilla, has been suggested, but in reality all these distinctive marks appear to be found only in Apollos. So that with Luther, and not a few modern scholars, we must either attribute it to him or give up the quest.

This statement is very sweeping, incorrect, and superficial. He does not even present the facts.

While we do not dogmatically assert our thesis of the Pauline authorship with any such note of certainty, we do not see fit to change our view without sufficient evidence. We still believe it to be reasonable to accept the Pauline tradition.

We deplore the fact that the King James Version carries the heading, *The Epistle of Paul the Apostle to the Hebrews*. It should read, *The Epistle to the Hebrews*. Such is the tenet that we affirm in this paper.

BIBLIOGRAPHY FOR APPENDIX

Calvin, John. *Commentary of Paul the Apostle on Hebrews*. 1567 Reprint. Grand Rapids, Michigan: Baker Book House, n.d.

Edwards, T. C. "The Epistle to the Hebrews," *Expositor's Bible*. Grand Rapids, Michigan: Baker Book House, n.d.

Gaebelein, Arno C. "The Epistle to the Hebrews," *The Annotated Bible*. Neptune, New Jersey: Loizeaux Brothers, n.d.

International Standard Bible Encyclopedia, article on the Epistle to the Hebrews. Grand Rapids, Michigan: Wm. B. Eerdmans Publishing Co., 1925.

Lindsay, W. *Lectures on The Epistle to the Hebrews*. *International Critical Commentary*. Edinburgh, Scotland: T. & T. Clark, 1867.

Moffatt, James. "The Epistle to the Hebrews," *International Critical Commentary*. Edinburgh, Scotland: T. & T. Clark, 1924.

Plumer, William. *Commentary on Paul's Epistle to the Hebrews*. Carlisle, Pennsylvania: The Banner of Truth, n.d.

Wickham, E. C. *Epistle to the Hebrews*. London, 1910.

BIBLIOGRAPHY

(Recommended for Further Study)

Bruce, F. F. *The Epistle to the Hebrews*. Grand Rapids, Michigan: Wm. B. Eerdmans Publishing Co., 1964.

DeHann, M. R. *Hebrews*. Grand Rapids, Michigan: Zondervan Publishing House, 1959. (Message given on the Radio Bible Class)

English, E. Schuyler. *Studies in the Epistle to the Hebrews*. Neptune, New Jersey: Loizeaux Brothers, 1955.

Hoyt, Herman A. *The Epistle to the Hebrews*. Winona Lake, Indiana: Brethren Missionary Herald Co., n.d.

Hughes, Philip Edgecumbe. *A Commentary on the Epistle to the Hebrews*. Grand Rapids, Michigan: Wm. B. Eerdmans Publishing Co., 1977.

Ironside, H. A. *The Epistle to the Hebrews*. Neptune, New Jersey: Loizeaux Brothers.

Kelly, William. *An Exposition of the Epistle to the Hebrews*. Addison, Illinois: Bible Truth Publishers, 1905.

Kent, Homer A., Jr. *The Epistle to the Hebrews*. Grand Rapids, Michigan: Baker Book House, 1972. (Excellent)

MacDonald, William. *The Epistle to the Hebrews*. Neptune, New Jersey: Loizeaux Brothers, 1971.

Meyer, F. B. *The Way into the Holiest*. Port Washington, Pennsylvania: Christian Literature Crusade, 1893. (A rich devotional study)

Murray, Andrew. *The Holiest of All*. Old Tappan, New Jersey: Fleming H. Revell Co., 1894. (Excellent devotional treatment)

Newell, William R. *Hebrews, Verse by Verse*. Chicago, Illinois: Moody Press, 1947. (Excellent)

Pfeiffer, Charles F. *The Epistle to the Hebrews*. Chicago, Illinois: Moody Press, 1962. (Good, brief survey)

Phillips, John. *Exploring Hebrews*. Chicago, Illinois: Moody Press, 1977.

Thomas, W. H. Griffith. *Hebrews: A Devotional Commentary*. Grand Rapids, Michigan: Wm. B. Eerdmans Publishing Co., 1962. (Excellent)

Vine, W. E. *The Epistle to the Hebrews*. London: Oliphant, 1957.

Wiersbe, Warren W. *Be Confident*. Chicago, Illinois: Moody Press, 1977.

Wuest, Kenneth S. *Hebrews in the Greek New Testament for English Readers*. Grand Rapids, Michigan: Wm. B. Eerdmans Publishing Co., 1947.